PERSPECTIVES

PERSPECTIVES

by

CHARLES W. GILKEY
Dean of Chapel, University of Chicago

With an Introduction by

ROBERT R. WICKS
Dean of Chapel
Princeton University

1933
Harper & Brothers Publishers
NEW YORK AND LONDON

Perspectives

To My Father and Mother
First Among My Religious Teachers

Acknowledgments

The sixth sermon in this volume, "Religion as Refuge—and as Challenge," appeared in the "Christian Century Pulpit" for June, 1930. The tenth sermon has been included with two other addresses in a symposium on "Life after Death," published as a pamphlet by the American Institute of Sacred Literature. The sermon on "Spiritual Understanding" was printed by the Westminster Congregational Church in London after it was preached in that pulpit. Parts of the sermon on "Refining Religion" were included in the sermon preached at the inauguration of President E. H. Wilkins at Oberlin, and afterward published by the college as there delivered, under the title "Education and Religion."

Contents

Introduction

We are emerging from an arid state of mind which put too much faith in explanations. We essayed to keep all our eggs in that one basket; and whatsoever could not be contained therein we took to be unreal, so much "sound and fury signifying nothing." Explanations still have their rightful claim, but appreciations once more demand their ancient place within our scheme of things. We know more than we can analyze. If we dissect our human nature to understand its elemental parts and inner workings, we will still believe that our best knowledge of a man comes from living with him before he is dissected. Scientists are warning us that whatever meaning life may have, it will not be found by taking life to pieces. Young atheists, who trust nothing reason cannot analyze, find relief in art, where beauty claims them by some direct awareness which no logic can explain. Since we were first pitched upon this strange planet and faced with this besetting, self-revealing reality all around us, life has proceeded by some dim appreciation first making us aware of all that lures us on to deeper understanding. By sheer living we grow conscious of a wealth of meaning and significance, which sustains, inspires, restores us, and has power to keep alive the seeking mind which "cannot bear not to know what could be known." This is why a certain mystic note is becoming dominant in our analytic age, grown just a little tired of explanations.

This book of sermons is in full accord with this fine trust in our best appreciations. The writer's method is poetic and suggestive, reminding us of age-old intuitions that

INTRODUCTION

have kept our race moving out beyond the paths of least resistance, where the finite fringes into the infinite, and man's uncertain will is caught and held by loyalty that feels a higher claim than his fellow men can make upon him. Our deeper sensitivity has been benumbed by the crude and ruthless beating of our cynical contemporaries. Our hypocrisies no doubt deserved the scourging. But now we are turning from the empty cisterns of a superficial age to the ancient wells at which our race has quenched its thirst and learned that "God is what we live by."

In parables, and pictures, and living stories of real people, Dean Gilkey deals with those tempers and misunderstandings which have made us unreceptive. The confusion of false perspectives, the suspicions of wishful thinking, the wrong measuring of values, deadness to old formulae, failure to discriminate between truth and the "earthen vessels" that convey it, the sense of futility,—these are the points at which the reader is met with hints that reconnect him with the best insight which our human heritage has given. And all is summed up in that most suggestive treatment of "Religion as Refuge—and as Challenge." A reading of this book would do much if it did no more than recover for the reader the wistful, fruitful, childlike mood of free appreciation.

ROBERT RUSSELL WICKS

Dean of the Chapel
Princeton University.

x

PERSPECTIVES

I

Across the valley from Stead's Ranch in Estes Park, in the heart of the Colorado Rockies, is one of the most perfect lateral moraines in the world. Some prehistoric glacier, bearing down within its slow ice-current the rocky debris of the higher ranges, has pushed that debris out into a long level ridge along what was once its flank, and left it there. So does a snow-plow push out and pile up a snow-bank along the sidewalk—except that here it is the plow that has melted, and the bank that has remained. So does a transatlantic liner push out from its moving prow a steady wave of curling white and translucent green: but here it was the glacier that was once white and green, and the moraine has remained to this day a pile of rock and rubble. The centuries since have covered it, first with a surface of soil, and then with a thicker mantle of dark-green pines. From our summer cabin across the valley that long, steep, pine-clad ridge was the most conspicuous foothill in our foreground.

Beyond and above the foothill lay the monarch of the whole range, Long's Peak, with its castle-like summit, more than 14,000 feet high. But the line of vision from our cabin across to the top of that ridge, and on beyond to the high shoulder of the Peak, was such that from our side of the valley we could see only the last thousand feet of the summit in the background above the moraine in the foreground, and so had little realization of the height or mass of Long's Peak. The foothill had largely obscured and completely minimized the mountain behind it.

The truer perspectives and relative altitudes of the region never really dawned on us until we motored up over

Deer Ridge, which lies back of our cabin along the side of the valley opposite the moraine, and rises a thousand feet higher. From its crest the huge mass of Long's Peak seemed to wall out half the southern sky, and the moraine that had loomed so large from the valley below had now shrunk to the foothill that it really was. Even more revealing was our experience when, some days later, we climbed 5,000 feet to the summit of Deer Mountain, made the magnificent perspectives of the whole range our own by the slow, hard-breathing attainment of an adequate altitude foot by foot, and so earned the mountaineer's exultant right to look with level eyes across all the foothills into the very face of the giants around him, and up with silent awe to the highest of them all—while the cars crawled like insects, and the moraine lay like a long wrinkle, in the valley far below.

The moraine and the mountain, in their relations each to the other, symbolize one of the most universal and perplexing problems of life in the modern world, a problem the difficulty and urgency of which increase for most of us with every passing year. It is the problem of perspective between the moraines and the mountains of life, of proportion between its details and its primacies. The current of modern life, utterly unlike the slow-moving glacier in its ever-accelerating rate of speed, is nevertheless like it in this, that it carries along within itself a steadily increasing mass of multitudinous detail, which piles up in a long lateral moraine beside all the margins of our living. In the valley where we spend most of our days these details bulk large and high, until they minimize or shut out of sight the higher ranges, less conspicuous, but far grander, that lie in the background. Only when we climb to these higher outlooks can we see how they dwarf into foothills the moraines that until now we had thought were mountains.

Part of this difficulty in keeping perspective arises, of course, from the steadily increasing tempo of modern life. The higher and higher speed of our trains, our automobiles, and our airplanes has set a new pace for all our living, and we are all getting into the confirmed speedster's habit of estimating the interest and significance of our journeys in terms of miles per hour—motion for its own sake—rather than in terms of a destination which justifies the journey. A prominent lawyer, who came some time ago from a down-state city to live and work in Chicago, remarked recently that at last he had caught on to being a Chicagoan: he had jumped up from the circle of his law-books, rushed out the office door and into the elevator, and then down the street half a block, before he stopped to ask himself, "Just where was I going, anyway?" As individuals and as a civilization we know less and less definitely where we are going, but we are on our way at higher speed. We have built a boulevard round the moraine for our high-powered cars—but the foothill hides the mountain even more completely from a driver than from a pedestrian.

A still greater difficulty in keeping perspective arises from the steadily increasing complexity of our interests and relationships. Our fathers in their simpler farm and village life worked, as a rule, far longer hours than we do: but at the end of the long day they were too tired with manual labor, and there were too few near neighbors or common pursuits, to leave their own fireside. Many of them at a family altar each morning, and more in church on Sundays, made it a regular practice to "lift up their eyes unto the hills." So, though their lives were filled with what we should call drudgery, they did find ways and times for climbing to see beyond and above it.

But with us, their children, a strange thing has happened. Most of us, week in and week out, have far more leisure from our major responsibilities than they ever dreamed of. But improved methods of transportation have put us within easy reach of hundreds of friends and thousands of neighbors, and of accessible and attractive opportunities for recreation. The multiplication of printed matter has deluged our attention with a flood of material, not all of which deserves the time it claims; and on Sunday mornings, when our fathers were accustomed to "turn their thoughts to higher things," our indolent laps and minds are filled with that miscellaneous mass of mediocrity, the Sunday newspaper. Improved communication by mail and telephone has multiplied our contacts with friends and neighbors, and the increase in our active interests and movings about in travel and on vacation has greatly multiplied the number of friends with whom we want to keep in touch. As a result of these and many other sources of accumulation of detail and debris, the moraines have mounted higher and higher about our daily living, till many of us can hardly see Long's Peak at all. Nor is the problem solved by the landscape-gardening of the moraine, no matter how skilfully done; flower-beds in the foreground of life can never fully take the place of mountains in its background.

Still more serious does the situation become when the habit of dead-level preoccupation in the shadow of the moraine dulls our sense for distinctions of depth and height, and quantity takes the place of quality as the dimension of life with which we are chiefly concerned. A professor of political science in a university located in a great city told me recently of a conversation with one of his students who on primary day had cut all his classes to work at the polls on behalf of the city's most notorious and unscrupulous political machine. When he asked this student how he could square this political affiliation with what the course had revealed concerning conditions in the city, he was staggered by this reply: "Well, there isn't any difference between right and wrong any longer, is there? And I needed the twenty bucks. What difference does it make who gave them to me?"

Even where the sense of moral distinctions has not flattened out quite so completely as that, the maintenance of its sensitiveness and effective control over conduct is dependent upon the frequent vision of higher ranges of living that both challenge and humble us, and upon the possession of enough energy and enthusiasm for climbing to lift us far enough above the dead levels of mediocrity and indifference to recognize that these are definitely "beneath us." The moral confusion and bewilderment of our post-war world is indeed partly due to the break-down of our traditional moral codes and the disintegration of their theological presuppositions and sanctions, as Walter Lippmann has so clearly pointed out; but in part also it is due to the blurring of our sense for this vertical third dimension in human experience, and the weakening of the climber's impulse and ambition in ourselves as individuals and in our society. Our generation does not see the heights or depths of life clearly enough to care particularly about climbing thither, or to fear either a slip or a fall. So we live precariously in an ethically flattened world.

American college life reflects increasingly the characteristics of the life outside our institutions of learning, as the number of students in our colleges from all groups in our population has increased so rapidly since the war, and as the points of interaction between American life and college life have been greatly multiplied thereby. As an inevitable result, the confusion among details and loss of salient perspectives with which we are so familiar in the larger area have been more and more evident as life has grown more complex in the smaller sector also. One of the leading school superintendents of the country, telling recently of his experiences as a graduate student in one of our great universities, remarked that new facts and points of view had been heaped upon him there every day in such bewildering profusion that one of his chief personal problems had been to avoid being intellectually buried alive—or at the very least to escape mental indigestion. He had found it helpful, he said, to seek out the quiet seclusion of certain neighborhood churches that were open during the week, in order there to think through the readjustment of his own attitudes and perspectives to the new facts that were piling up before him. His predicament, more, perhaps, than his procedure, is typical of our modern world.

The same problem in another and more urgent form confronts every student in an American college today. The bewildering variety and over-organization of its extra-curricular "college life"—the high-piled moraine of student activities and interests that fills the foreground of undergraduate attention—conceals behind its detail those higher but less conspicuous standards and qualities of life which "higher" education ought to disclose to all its beneficiaries. An observant dean remarked recently of one of the most prominent and popular undergraduates on an over-organized campus, that he was doing so many things that, without realizing it, he was forming the habit of doing none of them well. Another observer on that same campus points out that while abundant opportunity is provided for the transmission and acquisition of facts, far less help is given in the much more difficult and important task of readjusting attitudes and perspectives. The American college reflects our national tendency to lose sight of the mountain behind the moraine.

In the realm of religion this tendency is equally marked, and its results are not less serious. The slow-moving stream of organized religion always accumulates and carries down the generations an enormous mass of ceremonial, tradition, and creed, which it then deposits in a high-piled ecclesiastical moraine along the flank of contemporary religious life. Those church people who live all the time in the shadow of denominational detail of organization and ceremony—those whom Jesus once described as tithing mint and anise and cummin, and whom he could find today debating the validity of ordinations and measuring the amount of water to be used in baptism—are always in danger, like their predecessors, of forgetting the weightier matters, justice and mercy and faith. They too often lose their perspective for the great central verities of religion, missing God Himself behind the foothills of their own dogmatisms and ecclesiasticisms, and speaking arrogantly in His name without ever realizing how petty their presumption looks to those who have caught even a glimpse, above and beyond them, of what the New Testament calls "the majesty of God." Nor is this perennial danger limited to ecclesiastical and ceremonial controversy alone. It must be guarded against in all the ambitious efforts of our finite minds to define and explain in our theologies that third dimension of our human experience which extends upward toward the Infinite that lies always within our outreach, but never fully within our grasp. "If theorists would vindicate religion, they may do so: but religion comes forth in the majesty of silence, like a mountain amid the lifting mists."

It is the more important that religion should not lose its way among its own foothills, because, at its best and in the lives of its great masters, it has always been carried quickly to the upper ranges of human experience, and has there proved itself a sensitive and discriminating instrument for surveying the higher and the highest summits. It is striking to see how frequently and explicitly Jesus dealt with the problem of perspectives among values that are lower and higher. The study of his "firsts" is most rewarding. "Seek ye *first* . . . and all these things shall be added unto you." "This is the *first* and great commandment. And the second is like unto it." "What shall it profit a man, if he shall gain the whole world, and lose his own soul?" The story of Mary and Martha is a study in comparative values that

9

the world will never forget, and that neither a hostess nor a friend can afford to neglect, because it clears up certain perspectives about which our modern world is very much confused. We must notice that in none of these familiar cases did Jesus condemn or disparage the values that he explicitly rated as lower. He was no ascetic, denying "these things" any place in his scheme of life. Religion at its best never says that the detail and routine of life are unnecessary or unimportant; it only maintains, as Jesus always did, that they are secondary to things more important, and gain their own largest significance from the contribution they may make as means toward the realization of the highest ends. At no point do we modern folk more need the help of religion than in our contemporary confusion among values some of which are more important and some less. It is a main function of religion, in the life both of individuals and of society, to help us put first things first, and then, even at cost, to keep them there.

What can be done when we have stayed so long, as individuals or as a generation, in the valley of mediocrity or in the shadow of the moraine of detail and routine, that we have lost sight of the higher ranges, and even our ambition for climbing toward them? For one thing, life itself has a way of coming unexpectedly to our deliverance when we have grown short-sighted and low-hearted among the foothills. More swiftly even than in a powerful motor-car, we are borne now and then through some breath-taking and perhaps tragic experience to a point of vision where the depths open suddenly beneath us, and the heights reveal themselves far overhead. Browning knew well enough what some of these revealing experiences are:

> Just when we are safest, there's a sunset-touch,
> A fancy from a flower-bell, some one's death,
> A chorus-ending from Euripides. . . .

But these sudden glimpses of beauty or of tragedy which he names are not the only vistas which lift us into life's third dimension. A sophisticated student, graduating from college, falls deeply in love, or enlists for service in a great cause, or tackles a hard job, or hunts for one in vain, or when he marries finds himself presently face to face with responsibilities or anxieties that alter his entire outlook on life and make him smile a bit at the lack of perspective that he now begins to sense in his earlier undergraduate philosophizing. When any of us are threatened with the loss of health, or resources, or loved ones, we rarely see life thereafter as flatly as we viewed it before.

Our own generation is passing through experiences, some of them tragic, that have this same revealing quality. Our perspective on war, for instance, is altering fast and far. Even though the memory of its horrors under modern conditions may be somewhat dimmed with the passing of those who survived them, the realization of its futility and stupidity, and of the dangerous threat of such violence on our modern scale to the very structure of our civilization, is radically altering our attitude toward it. The world-wide depression, of which the war is certainly one major cause, is likewise bringing about profound changes in our perspectives, especially in this country. We Americans had been measuring life very largely in terms of the abundance of the things which we possessed, and had thought that we could indefinitely enlarge and enrich both it and ourselves by the competitive and acquisitive pursuit of "improved means toward an unimproved end." Now we begin to see that on that road disaster awaits us all, and that in an interdependent world such as ours has become, we can neither secure nor keep the individual means of life, unless we learn how to subordinate and devote them to the common ends of life. Whether our civilization will plunge to its destruction in the depths below, or climb toward larger human welfare on the heights above, who knows? But at least, in this year of grace and destiny numbered 1932 A.D., we can see both this peril and this possibility more clearly than we ever saw them before—and we know, too, that we cannot long tarry on the precarious path where now we hesitate.

But we can never rely solely on unexpected experiences, whether sublime or tragic, to clarify and renew our perspectives. The motor or the gasoline-tank we had relied on to carry us to the summit may fail—or no passing car may come to give us a lift when we need it most. Just as the best views and steadiest perspectives are gained in the mountains by those who have trained themselves to climb thither foot by foot, so the surest and steadiest perspectives on life are gained by those who have disciplined themselves in the art and practice of spiritual mountaineering. Public worship is such an art and practice. Those who "drop into church occasionally," without finding or seeing much there when they arrive, have forgotten that one does not drop into or slide on to a mountain summit. Even more is private prayer such an art and practice. Under the conditions and distractions of modern life, the great insights and inclusive outlooks have to be sought and struggled for upon a difficult trail of meditation, communion, and consecration, which religion has slowly learned to climb, with upreached hand and bended knee.

WISHFUL THINKING *in* RELIGION

II

The poet who penned this couplet, as he looked back over
the religious history of his forefathers, had never heard of
wishful thinking. He never had to face the question which
our own generation, beginning to see how easily human
nature can fool itself into believing what it wants to believe
and then find reasons for it afterward, has had to ask about
religious faith. Is it then humanity's most egregious case
of wishful thinking on a cosmic scale? Is religion the projection, into an ideal world beyond this one, or another life
after this one, of what human nature very much wants but
can't manage to get here and now? Does religion project
into the nature of God those qualities of mind and heart,
those adequacies of will, those cosmic guarantees and cer-
tainties, which men seek in vain within and among themselves, and therefore want all the more to find somewhere?
Are we simply rationalizing, or rather sanctifying our own
deepest desires, as Lytton Strachey with his ruthless dis-
section has shown us that certain "Eminent Victorians"
sometimes did, when we justify these desires by calling
them the will of God?

Last Christmas a mystery play in the mediæval manner
was given in the chancel of the University of Chicago
Chapel. The footlights, concealed behind the chancel rail,
threw against the reredos huge magnified shadows from the
moving shepherds, wise men, and angels in the foreground;

15

and no small part of the fascination of the play came from watching those mysterious shadows on that gigantic scale. Is religion in human experience like those gigantic shadows —mysterious and fascinating to be sure, but after all just a projection of our own human desires against a cosmic screen?

With these characteristic modern questions there has come also for our generation the related and familiar question, is religion then an escape from reality into this dream-world of our wishful imagining? When we worship and when we pray, are we running away to a beautiful place and a quiet hour, out of a real world that is too rough for us? And is what we call religious experience only a soothing compensation in this ideal world, for what we cannot manage or achieve in the real one?

We modern folk have the advantage of the Psalmist in that we live in a generation when these questions have been raised by our psychology, and have to be faced by our religion. For they make it all too plain that a great deal of religion, both historical and contemporary, has fallen victim to this danger of wishful thinking and this temptation to compensating escape. It is a real service to the cause of sound religion to have this danger clearly pointed out. Religion comes to us down the generations along a highroad beside which, on either hand, lie these dangerous ditches into which it may fall at any moment if its contemporary drivers grow careless or fall asleep at the wheel. Our own generation has located these ditches and realized their constant peril more clearly than did its predecessors, and ought to be able, therefore, more surely to stay out of them. Many of us would agree that even in our own time these ditches of wishful thinking and flight from reality have claimed many a religious victim. We were taught to sing as children:

When all my labors and trials are o'er
And I am safe on that beautiful shore,
Just to be with the dear Lord I adore
Will through the ages be glory for me.

From the standpoint of our later years the perspectives and attitudes of that once popular "Glory Song" are not only seriously less than Christian, but contain obvious elements of wishful thinking and compensating escape.

Any religion that minimizes the importance or denies the reality of evil and sickness and death in our human lot, of human ignorance and folly and sin in determining our human fate, needs this perpetual warning against the dangers of wishful thinking. So does any religion that half-consciously or unconsciously compensates for its intellectual or ethical inadequacies by claiming infallibility for its creed or its authorities, or priority in the world to come for its adherents. Every human interest has certain temptations or vices to which it is peculiarly exposed. Provinciality, complacency, and superiority are the familiar besetting sins of religion, especially in its organized expression; and a sharp warning against wishful thinking is a needed safeguard against these perennial temptations.

When this contant danger has once been frankly recognized, we shall then be in a position to discover that the same modern psychology which warned us against these perils assures us also that the best safeguard against wishful thinking is by no means to stop thinking altogether, but rather to turn our thinking in the right direction. Human thought and desire may move in either of two directions: *away* from reality toward vain wishes that may become daydreams and finally delusions into which one escapes; or *toward* reality, as the mind and will grapple with the real world, striving to understand and solve its problems, unlock its secrets, and master its difficulties. The latter direction, that of realistic as opposed to "autistic" or "dereistic" thinking, has not only given us all our inventions from boats to airships, but our applied sciences and modern techniques as well. There are those who tell us that along this road the human mind itself has developed. The urgent question, therefore, always is, Which way is your thinking moving?

So is it also with the ambiguous word "escape." There are certain ways of escape from the realities of life that are dangerous because they are too risky: escape with a needle into the dream-world of drugs; escape with a bottle into the drunken world of intoxication; escape with a delusion into the crazy world of insanity. There are other escapes from reality which the best moral sense of humanity condemns as cowardly—running away from a job because it is hard, or a duty because it is difficult, or a responsibility that others are depending on us to carry. Suicide is such an escape; running away, it leaves others to clean up the mess and carry on.

But, on the other hand, there are escapes from reality that normal human experience shows to be indispensable for healthy and effective living. Such is the escape of sound sleep every night; of physical exercise and mental recreation every day; of a change of scene and air now and then, and a vacation at least once a year. The penalty of neglecting such necessary escapes is physical and nervous breakdown, as our own generation has discovered to its cost. Art, literature, music, hobbies, are similar ways of indispensable escape; so are plays and fiction, and that favorite escape of the overworked professorial mind—a good detective story! All these send us back toward reality after a period of release and refreshment, ready to face it anew and more successfully.

So also is it with religion. Those who tell us that the best way to avoid wishful thinking in religion is to abandon religion altogether, are not following their own argument through. Everything depends on what kind of religion it is —and that in turn on the direction in which it is moving.

18

If it is fleeing from the world in cowardly or compensatory escape, seeking thrills for itself in an orgy of sentimentality or a dream of bliss, it is poor religion. But if, in the quiet of its meditation, through the clearer perspectives disclosed to its worship and its prayer, by the rededication of itself to causes and purposes greater than its own self-centered satisfaction, it is clearing its vision, renewing its courage, and strengthening its will to face the world and transform it, then it is good religion. The classic utterance of the Christian religion, truer to its characteristic spirit and attitude than any creedal statement can ever be, is the Lord's Prayer. "Thy will be done on earth as it is done in heaven." There is religion at its best; its eyes lifted to heaven to find its bearings and direction; its feet on the ground where its life has to be lived; its hands stretched out toward its next task.

We may seem at this point to be a long way from the Hebrew poet with whose couplet we started as our text; but we are not nearly so far as we may think. To be sure, he had never heard of wishful thinking or its dangers for religion; and yet he at least, in spite of his ignorance of these matters, did not need our modern warning against these dangers. He had found a religious road that led him far and high above these dangers: a steep road and a hard one, but climbing rapidly away from the mirages and ditches of the valley and following the crests. Did you notice what he declared to be the trouble with his forefathers? They desired certain things very much, and tried to use their religion as a means for getting them. They got what they wanted, but in so doing they tempted God, for they were wanting the wrong things. To put his prophetic insight into our own modern speech, religion at its best is much more than a technique for getting the things we want, or even for making the world over into what we want it to become. It involves a constant reference to a

Purpose greater and worthier than our own, described beyond and above us, dimly understood; by which, nevertheless, our own desires and purposes must be perpetually revised and corrected—to which, as it emerges, we ourselves are forever dedicated. That is one element among several in a theistic faith without which sound religion would be seriously impoverished. To describe religion, as some of our contemporaries superficially do, as if it were simply wishful thinking, a short cut to getting what we want by persuading God to gratify our desires, is to see only the low road of religion with its dangerous ditches plain on either side, and to draw all our conclusions about religion from the fate of those who do indeed too often land in the ditch or the swamp. A generation as indisposed as our own toward strenuous moral and social effort, and as indolent as our own in spiritual mountain-climbing, is likely entirely to miss the religious trails that in every generation have led its more adventurous spirits up out of the valley to a highroad along the crest.

This text has been chosen chiefly in the hope that it may give us glimpses here and there of this highroad, as religion at its best has followed it down the generations. It is plain to see in the text itself. The people had cared chiefly for the comforts of a full stomach, and the poet declares that God gave them what they wanted—but it was not what God cared most about at all, and getting what they wanted proved in the end disastrous, because they wanted the wrong thing. Another glimpse of the same road in Hebrew history appears in Amos' warning to his contemporaries. They had thought that in the great day of the Lord they would get what they wanted, because they were already giving God what he wanted—solemn feasts and rich sacrifices. Amos told them that the day of the Lord would be darkness and not light, a day of judgment, because what God wanted was social justice, and they, too, were wanting the wrong things. More clearly yet does the same highroad appear in Jesus' answer to James and John when they asked for the chief seats in his coming kingdom; and most clearly and poignantly of all under the trees in Gethsemane. "Not my will but Thine be done." On his knees in the garden, Jesus came to see that he had been asking for the wrong thing, and that he was being guided into another pathway than the one he would himself have chosen.

Nor is that highroad an ancient one alone. We modern liberals often quote the faith of the Pilgrims who were expecting "more light and truth to break forth from God's holy word"; but we do not so often recall their declared purpose to follow together, not only his ways already made known to them, but his ways still to be made known. We find it much easier to liberalize our theology than to Christianize our way of life. Perhaps the most memorable signpost pointing toward this road in American history is Abraham Lincoln's reply to the delegation of ministers who came asking him during the darkest days of the Civil War whether he was sure that God was on their side. His answer was that what gave him much more concern was the question whether they were on God's side! "The Almighty has His own purposes," and they were different from those of either party in the great conflict. It was an insight akin to that of Phillips Brooks in his well-known counsel about prayer. "Oh, do not pray for easier lives; pray to be stronger men. Do not pray for tasks equal to your powers; pray for powers equal to your tasks."

To borrow a term from contemporary European politics, religion at its best is always revisionist. It bids men revise and revise yet again, not only their thoughts of God as these show themselves to be inadequate in the light of advancing knowledge and deepening insight, but also and no less the direction of their living, as His greater and worthier purposes are more fully made known to them.

All this has important consequences in confused and changing times like our own. Is our generation in its present serious difficulties partly at least because we too have tempted God by wanting the wrong things? Significantly enough, it was not the preacher Fosdick, but his lawyer brother, who at the recent dedication of the Oriental Museum at the University of Chicago raised some searching questions about our modern civilization which the *New York Times* then asked him to put into writing as a "tremendous challenge" to mankind at the beginning of 1932.

At this moment, in the midst of our economic depression, we are praying for the return of prosperity. What do we mean by prosperity? Do we mean the shrieking, high-power salesmanship and the fever of stimulated wants that made up the whole of existence before 1929? Do we mean a society of patterned minds in which every man desires whatever his neighbor has, and life is a hectic scramble for gadgets and knick-knacks? It seems inconceivable that anyone would want to go back to such a condition. There must be something better.

We were all of us caught in a system which was not of our making and which we could not control. Now it has broken down. Are we merely to patch it up so that we can live as we lived before? Surely if prosperity means only houses and furniture and automobiles and radios and telephones and all the other paraphernalia of living—and no life that transcends all these mechanisms—then we should earnestly pray that the blight of prosperity may never return.

The remark of Lincoln Steffens, as he looked out on a world to which another great war will bring irreparable disaster, points the same question: "None of us wants war —but all of us want things that we can't have without war." Our young men, like the young men of Israel long ago, will be smitten down—and our civilization with them—unless we revise our perspectives so that our desire for peace comes decisively ahead of our desire for the things that cannot be had without war.

So this old text, like the flashlight in the hand of the

doctor as he examines our throat to see how serious is the infection there, becomes a social and spiritual flashlight searching into the thoughts and intents of our own hearts. An alternative marginal rendering gives a memorable turn to its final phrase:

> "They tempted God in their heart
> By asking food *for themselves*."

Will the historians of two or three centuries hence, looking back on the breakdown of what we now call our modern civilization, say of the well-educated men and women of our generation what the Psalmist said of his predecessors? They tempted God by asking for themselves, when they left college, a good living, a comfortable suburban detachment from the burdens of their generation, an armchair sophistication, in days when the destinies of their civilization were hanging in the balance.

"They tempted God. . . and he gave them their own desires."

Is RELIGION a FROZEN ASSET?

III

Two magazines that came to my desk within the same month have raised this question. One of them was concerned about the urgent human needs which have to be met in every American city this winter, and asked whether, at a time when so many financial resources are frozen up tight, religion can prove itself something better than one more frozen asset. The other article was even more concerned about the threat of another great war that hangs over against our modern world somewhat as Vesuvius, with its threat of cloud by day and fire by night, must have hung over against the doomed city of Pompeii nineteen hundred years ago. What, this writer asked, can be done to avert that threatened eruption and the doom that it will bring to our civilization? Can religion do anything? Or is it, like so many other resources that we have lately found unavailable in our time of greatest need, just one more frozen asset?

Most of us have learned during the last two years what the question means. Before 1929, unless we were very familiar with financial terms, we had never particularly noted the significant word "liquid" that has long been used to describe those assets of a bank or a business that can quickly be turned into cash without serious loss, because there is always a ready market for them at something like their intrinsic values. But in these last two years, as the temperature of public confidence has gone down and farther down, until shivers of apprehension have stiffened into the paralyzing grip of fear, we have seen assets of all kinds that had lately been liquid freeze up tight. The other day I heard the now familiar story in a new setting: this time about a Chicagoan who in 1929 owned over a million dollars' worth of valuable farm lands in the central west and of mining properties in the Rockies. A letter from his wife to one of their neighbors had just brought word that they are living by themselves in a little cabin on one of their claims, hoping for patience and courage to hold on through the winter there in the mountains, because there isn't a single one of their holdings that is under present conditions convertible into cash. Frozen assets! Substantial values there, beyond question—if only the owners can hang on through this hard winter until these assets thaw out and become liquid again.

So is it not only with mortgage loans that banks or individuals may have made on any number of intrinsically valuable properties like these; so is it also with the motor cars and boats, the pianos and paintings that any of us may happen to own—most of all with the stocks that may be selling today almost as far below their real value as in 1929 they were selling above it. To have to dispose of them at present prices is little less than tragic, for they possess values that can't be realized on at the moment. Hence the now familiar phrases: frozen assets, frozen credit, frozen capital. As one of the two magazine editorials points out, all these physical properties are intrinsically just about what they were a year or two ago. It is the intangibles that have frozen up tight: the imponderables of mutual confidence, general demand, sense of social stability that always make up so large a part of the value of anything. Our only real hope lies in the release which a returning springtime of general confidence will surely bring again sooner or later, when the streams of trade begin to move and rise once more, and the ice breaks up at last and goes out to sea.

Now our present question is whether all this has happened to religion also in our modern world. The first and obvious answer is that it may happen to religion at any time, and that it has happened in our time to certain kinds

28

of religion in the possession of certain groups of people. What the song calls "that old-time religion" used once to circulate at what might be called spiritual par in that old-time world whose ways of thinking and sense of values it so largely shared. There are plenty of people in the world today of whom and for whom this is still true, and they find the "old-time religion" still a liquid spiritual asset, on which they can and do "cash in" for faith and hope, for conscience and courage to meet their own crises of spiritual need. But there is a rapidly increasing multitude of people in our modern world, including the overwhelming majority of the college-trained younger generation, for whom this is no longer the case. The fundamental assumptions of "that old-time religion" about the universe of which we are a part, about this world and another world, about God and man and their relations, about the nature and the fact of revelation, about the person of Christ and the authority of the Bible—assumptions that were widely taken for granted in the thinking of an earlier day—are no longer convincing either for their thinking or their living. In this new intellectual climate of the modern world the traditional doctrines not only of Christianity, but of all the great historic religions, have been more and more heavily discounted as these new ways of thinking have made their influence more and more widely felt. As an inevitable result, a great many modern folk don't know whether to list religion as an asset or a liability, personal and social, or whether to throw it away as worthless. For the present at least it is to them a frozen asset.

Nor is this experience limited to the intellectual perplexities about religion that confuse students and graduates of our colleges. It happens almost as often to individuals and families who move from the simpler life of smaller towns and cities, where certain religious relationships and attitudes have been widely taken for granted, to the complicated and heterogenous world of our larger cities, and the sophistication of their suburbs. Finding a wide variety of points of view toward religion among their new neighbors, instead of the conformity which had been the accepted attitude among the old, freed from personal and financial responsibilities that they and perhaps their parents before them had long carried for the maintenance of organized religion—they find it easy enough to let their church letters lie in a trunk in the attic, or on the non-resident list of the old home church from which they couldn't think of asking for a transfer; and these dusty documents soon come to symbolize the current value of their religion as a going concern.

We have all realized these last few months that when in matters commercial too large a proportion of a community's assets are frozen, there ensues a panicky state of mind that itself becomes one of the most serious factors in the economic situation. Men lose their sense of security and confidence, weigh their judgment and initiative down with their panic fears until their craft wallow helplessly in the rough sea of the passing storm and too often sink to ruin, when with more courage and faith they might have shortened sail and made port. This happens in matters spiritual no less. It may very well be that the future historian of these disillusioned and cynical years since the Great War, will ascribe them not simply to the hard-headed realism of which we have been so proud, but also in part to a state of spiritual panic of which we have hardly been aware. The old but shrewd remark that a cynic is one who knows the price of everything but the value of nothing, takes on new meaning and point in days when some have talked and many have acted as if there were no moral and spiritual values left anywhere. If, as Mr. Joseph W. Krutch assures us, that is "the modern temper," we may profitably note that it is also very much like the temper of a panic. And just as we tell panicky hoarders, whose eyes are big with terror lest our economic order is going utterly to smash, that dark as things are their fears are making them see things at night, so may we not with equal fairness tell our contemporary "futilitarians" that whatever their current quotations on ethical and spiritual values, the moral order of the universe hasn't yet gone utterly to smash?

The parallel may fairly be followed even farther. If one happens to own a piece of real estate that until recently would have been accounted valuable, this is certainly a bad time to try to sell it: but it does not at all follow that the best thing to do is to give it away. The stocks and bonds in a safety-deposit box are most of them quoted nowadays at prices considerably less than when they were put there; but he would be a very foolish pessimist who on that account should tear them up. There are values in both that there is every reason to believe can be realized sooner or later, if meanwhile the owner can hold on through the present storm. Just so, in a time of spiritual destitution and panic like the present, when there is reason to believe that for lack of a faith to live for and live by, more people are starving in soul than in body; when society itself is threatened with moral bankruptcy for lack of ready reserves of conscience and character and consecration, built up by individual integrity and available in a social crisis—surely it is a time to say to everybody, younger or older, whose religion may at the moment be a frozen asset, *"Don't throw it away.* There are values there which you may not be able to realize just now—which it may take time and trouble to cash in on. But hold steady—and hang on."

That brings us to the deeper question which is our central concern today. What can one do about a personal religion that for whatever reason is at the moment frozen up? A working answer to that question will help us also on another question closely related and not less important. How can we keep our own religion from tightening up into a frozen asset?

The first step is plain to see from the ground we have

31

covered already. We must keep religion in constant contact and circulation with the best thinking of our time; we must keep our own personal religion in such contact and circulation with our own best thinking.

In my senior year in the seminary, our beloved president, Charles Cuthbert Hall, had just returned from his second series of Barrows lectures in the student centers in the Orient; and in my only personal talk with him in the brief interval between his return and his last illness, I raised the question that was just then perplexing several of us. Would we render the larger service by devoting our lives to teaching in the Far East, or to the parish ministry in America? His quick reply has come back to me a score of times through the twenty years since. He had come home from the Orient surer than ever, he said, that the religious crisis of our own generation was here in our own land. Religion in America was having to steer its difficult and perilous course between the Scylla of an unintelligent conservatism and the Charybdis of an unreligious liberalism. On the one side were the stout defenders of the old-time religion who had a gospel to declare, but did not know the language of their time—and so their age would not listen to them. On the other were the kind of liberals who knew the latest lingo perfectly, but had no gospel for the deeper needs of their generation. Could American Christianity find the narrow and tortuous channel between?

That is the first question to which religion in the modern world must find an answer if it is to keep itself available for the crises of modern life. Those of us who have watched some of our classmates in college try to keep a high-school boy's religion in one water-tight compartment within their experience, while their maturer thinking develops in another, have learned what to expect sooner or later when our neighbors and friends make the same precarious attempt in later years to partition life off into chambers that have no communication with one another. Inner tensions and fears develop that render one or another of the areas involved first impotent and finally unreal, or that may become acute enough to make the whole structure collapse from inner strain. And this can happen within religious groups as well. Rufus Jones tells of a minister who recently remarked that one difference between us and our fathers is that they sang

> When I survey the wondrous cross . . .

and then went out to turn their community upside down; whereas we make a series of elaborate surveys of our community—and then leave it very much as it was before!

This task of mastering the new techniques and ways of thinking, without losing the old dynamics, calls for much more, however, than epigrams or formulæ; it has to be worked, or rather *lived*, through in the slow-moving process of the life-experience of individuals and groups. That became plain in our various experiences as college classmates in the religious perplexities that are natural, if not inevitable, for growing minds in changing days like our own. Those who tried to keep their adolescent religion and their growing minds in separate compartments usually fell victims to a spiritual breakdown sooner or later. Others wore their doubts and difficulties a bit proudly, as if they were another kind of Phi Beta Kappa key, marking the intellectual superiority of the wearer. Both these groups of men were all too often unable to work their way through to any constructive religious faith integrated with the rest of their experience. Some, however, who sought a path not round or over their intellectual difficulties, but through them, found that path leading out at last into a positive faith of their own. Dean Sperry has reminded us that what the hymn calls "new thoughts of God" have ever since the days of Job been born out of travail of mind and soul alike; and that such travail, in the spiritual realm as in the physical, bears its high cost in pain. We shall not find our way

33

easily or cheaply to such new thoughts of God: but along this difficult road lies the first step toward keeping one's religion a liquid rather than a frozen asset in changing times like these.

A second step is even more fundamental. Religion at its deepest and best is not so much a formula for explaining the world or our experiences in it, as it is a dynamic for overcoming and transforming the world. If, therefore, religion is to be kept from hardening into a frozen asset, it must, like a hydraulic press, be kept constantly at work exerting moral leverage and spiritual pressure on our own lives and the life around us. A committee of the Board of Social Service and Religion at the University of Chicago, composed equally of faculty and students, met recently to draw up the list of visiting speakers to be invited to the university chapel for next year. After the faculty members had made their comments and suggestions, one of the seniors was asked by the chairman whom, in his judgment, the students wanted most to hear. He replied that he had been talking that question over with some of his mates, and found general agreement that they would be most interested in hearing at the chapel men like Reinhold Niebuhr and Norman Thomas, who could stand over against the life and standards of our modern world with a critical attitude that would help us locate what is wrong with them. The instinct of youth, that religion must help us find out what is wrong with ourselves and with our world, is a sound one. The note of judgment that looks upon things as they are from the standpoint of what they ought to be, has never long been silent in either the Hebrew or the Christian religion ever since the days of the Old Testament prophets; and one of the most hopeful signs about present-day religion is that after a period of easy-going complacency and optimism it is recovering this note of judgment and this deepening sense of sin, personal and social. Therein lies a second essential for keeping religion from becoming a frozen asset.

But the final word in this matter is one of encouragement rather than exhortation. When the ice breaks up and goes out of the northern lakes in the spring, our deepest source of confidence is in the returning sunshine above and beyond us, on the light and warmth of which all our human living is finally dependent. Such is also religion's ultimate dependence upon that final source of light and life, above and beyond all our human resources, which we mean when we say God. There is one aspect of this religious assurance which is especially good news—a real gospel, therefore—for dark days like these: it is the discovery that these greatest resources of religion are available and accessible when circumstances outwardly may seem to be at their worst. So Christian faith has always found in the very tragedy of Calvary its clearest revelation of the love and nearness of God, bringing good out of evil and overcoming evil with good.

That same assurance has always found God near at hand, even in the darkness. Long centuries ago a Hebrew poet wrote of the divine presence, "If I make my bed in hell, behold, Thou art there." Some of us in our younger days thought, with the hasty cocksureness of youth, that a verse like that must have lost most of its meaning, except in some antiquarian sense, for a modern world that no longer believes in a physical hell or a subterranean Sheol as the abode of departed spirits. But in our later years we have rediscovered a deep religious significance in that verse, quite apart from and far below all questions of its cosmological reference. We have walked the streets for hours with neighbors and dear friends who make their bed in hell every night—the hell of worry and fear over what the morrow may bring forth. "If I make my bed in hell, behold Thou art *there*." The religious assurance beneath those ancient words is no longer for us some cosmological or

35

philosophical doctrine of the divine omnipresence in the physical universe; it is the living faith of religion that even in the coldest winter and the darkest night, God is never beyond our human reach.

Our modern world has had striking evidence of this assurance in the religious experience of Francis Thompson. His "Hound of Heaven" is often called the greatest of modern religious poems. But the sense of God's unfailing presence that inspired it is not less vividly stated in those other lines found among his papers after his premature death, that tell plainly enough where the vision of God came to him. In the days of his desperate struggle with poverty as a medical student in London he sold matches on Charing Cross and slept nights on the Thames Embankment. The indifferent faces of the hurrying crowd that was too preoccupied with its own concerns to care about him or his matches, and the dull surface of the muddy river that flowed past the benches on which he slept, both reappear in these lines as the setting for the great discovery that transformed life for him and made him sure that the Kingdom of God is "in no strange land."

> 'Tis ye, 'tis your estranged faces,
> That miss the many-splendoured thing.
>
> But (when so sad thou canst not sadder)
>   Cry;—and upon thy so sore loss
> Shall shine the traffic of Jacob's ladder
>   Pitched betwixt Heaven and Charing Cross.
>
> Yea, in the night, my Soul, my daughter,
>   Cry,—clinging Heaven by the hems;
> And lo, Christ walking on the water,
>   Not of Genesareth, but Thames!

"BARNABAS . . . SON of ENCOURAGEMENT"

a cheerful companion

Encouragement.

IV

*"Joseph . . . whom the apostles had named
Barnabas, which means Son of Encouragement."*
—Acts IV:36, the American (Goodspeed)
Translation

The various renderings of this phrase in the different versions of the New Testament are like windows variously placed, each of which gives us its own distinctive outlook upon the life of the early church and the character of one of its leaders. "The son of consolation" is the King James translation. That window shows us a little group of humble folk facing great deprivations and dangers for the sake of their new-found faith; and among them a man of quick sympathy and deep assurance, who could console them in all their present losses with the prospect of speedy recompense. "Son of exhortation" is the American Revised rendering. That window discloses a little company meeting secretly from house to house; and among them a leader whose strong faith and moving eloquence could screw their courage and loyalty to the sticking-point. Professor Goodspeed has translated it "Son of Encouragement." That window shows us an inconspicuous fellowship of devoted men and women whose moral and spiritual convictions were nevertheless the seed of a great future; and among them a leader who could hearten their difficult present with the encouraging assurance that such seed, in the right soil with proper care under God's rain and sunshine, would bring forth thirty, sixty, even a hundredfold.

The word in the Greek original thus variously rendered into English carries all three meanings in different contexts: as if to suggest that religion likewise brings men all three of these great goods—consolation, exhortation, encouragement—according to their need at the moment. And this new name Barnabas, which the apostles gave to Joseph according to the Oriental custom that renamed a man in terms of his distinctive characteristics, reminds us of the power of religion to call forth and sustain previously undeveloped capacities in men which may become, as apparently in his case, the distinguishing characteristic of his matured personality. That this new name described him accurately to the end, the subsequent history of the early church abundantly shows: especially the revealing story in Acts XI of the encouragement he gave to the little group in Antioch where the disciples were first called Christians; and of the great influence which he plainly had over the formative period in the Christian experience of his greater fellow worker, Paul.

So much is ancient history. As we modern folk look back upon it, especially our younger generation, most of us are not particularly interested in Barnabas the Son of Consolation: we have very little desire, spiritually speaking, to have our hand held. Still less does Barnabas the Son of Exhortation appeal to our generation: less perhaps than any previous generation do we want to be preached to or at. But if Barnabas the Son of Encouragement will only appear among us in days like these, that would be a very different story. We have no small need of him. We are living in a time of depression that is not only financial, but moral and spiritual as well—a time when the common stock of human nature, under the pressure of a long-continued bear market engineered by a clever group of cynics and debunkers, has gone down and yet farther down until its current quotations are far below its true value, and still farther below its capacities as a going concern, as these values and capacities are revealed in the daily business of living. In such a time we greatly need some contemporary

Barnabases—Sons of Encouragement—who can do for a panicky moral and spiritual market what financiers with ready assets have more than once in recent months done for the stock market in a crisis. One of the main functions of religion in dark days like these is to steady and encourage the spiritual situation with such substantial underwriting and assurance from a personal religious faith.

The need for Barnabas, and the search for him, are both plain to see in more than one area of modern life. Some months ago Mr. Lee Wilson Dodd published in a New York column some verses entitled "Enough Sunset Gun—a Poem in Dispraise of Practically Nothing":

> It's quite the thing now to write verses
>   Like curses:
> Sophisticate bards thumb their noses
>   At roses,
> And sing that inconstancy vexes
>   The sexes,
> That life's a swindle and that dying
>   's worth trying.
> But to me while they're posing and frowning,
>   Old Browning
> Bursts heartily in with his cheering
>   Unfearing,
> With a blast from his slughorn like Roland
>   In woeland,
> And blows them away to Gehenna.
>   No senna
> Makes acrid the wine that he pours us.
>   He bores us
> At times with his basso robusto,
>   But gusto
> Is better at least than combining
>   With whining
> The wisecracks of Main street Manhattan.
>
> Roll that in your cigarette papers, you sneerers
>   At cheerers!

This same need for men whose spiritual name is Barnabas has been apparent also in recent years upon our college campuses. In a well-known eastern college recently I was invited by a group of serious-minded undergraduates to lead a discussion on "The Answer of Religion to Student Cynicism." I asked a member of the philosophy department whether he thought the subject a paper problem or a real one. His interesting reply was that he felt that a good deal of contemporary student cynicism was a pose, cultivated as a mark of superior intellectuality and sophistication; but that it would not last long because it is not a natural outlook on life for healthy-minded youth. More trenchant was the comment of the headmaster of one of the best-known eastern preparatory schools, that his school had never produced finer graduates than during the last few years—but that he was more and more distressed to see them go out into what he called "the flood of cheap cynicism" sweeping so strongly through the colleges. Another headmaster recently referred in a public address to what he called "the sophomoric mind now enjoying open season in the colleges"; and said that he regarded this as the consequence of an overdose of the natural sciences, coupled with a blindness to the values that are only revealed in human and social experience. There was even more acuteness in the analysis of a prominent lawyer who through the twenty-five years since his own graduation has lived close to the campus of a great university. He maintained that the recent development of the tutorial system has given a disproportionate influence over the undergraduate mind to men who themselves are only a few years out of college, who have had the misfortune to come to maturity during the period when the tide of post-war disillusionment has been at its lowest ebb, who have not yet been disciplined by responsibility and mellowed by a large experience of life—and who have transferred their own sophistication and cynicism straight to the impressionable mind of the undergraduate.

He believes that a sounder balance will ultimately come with the securing of abler and larger men for undergraduate instruction, and with the establishment of more contacts between the student and the outstanding personalities of the faculty. Meanwhile, however, he shared the anxiety recently expressed by the president of one of our great universities, lest in days like these students go forth from our colleges "cynical of human virtues and indifferent to the things of the spirit."

This contemporary climate in the colleges is of course not to be taken too seriously. Sometimes, as already suggested, it is more or less of a pose; it has been the contemporary college fashion of late to be hardboiled and disillusioned—and there is no area of American life where the fashion of the hour, whether in fur coats, galoshes, or opinions, holds more absolute sway than on most college campuses. There is in the situation also a wholesome reaction against the mass of propaganda of which we were all the victims during the war, and against the easy optimism and complacency that were so widely prevalent both before and after the war. The realism of contemporary student thinking is a hopeful sign of a better future, especially when it is lifted by the returning tide of a rising social and personal idealism that is now plainly in evidence among the students who are entering our colleges as their hard-boiled predecessors pass out. Too many causes have contributed to this complicated situation to make either its analysis or its cure a simple matter. The determination of realistically-minded youth to face the facts, and to have done with shams and pretensions, is full of promise for the future. Meanwhile, however, it is important to realize that the college campus, like every other area of human life, cannot live healthily or happily without the presence in its midst of some men whose *middle* name at least is Barnabas— Son of Encouragement.

Every first-class teacher, if he aim at more than the mere

43

impartation of facts and seeks to develop latent capacities as well, must have Barnabas at least for a spiritual middle name. It was my good fortune in my first two years in college to work in English composition under the guidance of two famous teachers of the art of writing. One of them used caustic irony as his constant instrument for the cutting and polishing of our rough English style. I can still feel the shivers of apprehension running down my freshman spine whenever the gleaming edge of that cutting weapon flashed in my direction—while every creative idea fled from my paralyzed mind, and my vocabulary shrank to stammers upon my trembling tongue. I have never much wondered that my work in that course received and doubtless deserved the lowest grade I had in college; and I finished that first year with no confidence and almost as little enthusiasm for writing. The next year I came under a teacher with a greater reputation, who could be even blunter with his criticism: but I shall never forget the change inside me on the day when he gave me his first word of encouragement. "Keep on—you're doing better." The world about me blossomed that day with subjects to write about, and inevitable adjectives and verbs thronged to the point of my pen. My grades in that course immediately began to show the stimulating influence of a teacher who understood the art of encouragement as well as of criticism. Every parent, like every teacher concerned for the development of latent capacity, knows that sunshine is at least as important in that process as a pruning-knife. Those of us who seek to develop social responsibility and religious attitudes among those who do not yet know their own deeper interests and capacities, can least of all dispense with Barnabas' gift of encouragement.

Our modern Barnabas is more effective, however, as a man of deeds than of words. He may lack the eloquence of Joseph among his early fellow Christians, provided he possess certain deeper secrets of kindling power. On a Saturday afternoon in early September, just before the finals in the national tennis championship at Forest Hills on Long Island, two old-timers play the final match in the veterans' tournament. The winner of the veterans' championship in 1929 was a man forty-five years old. Much more significant than his age, however, was the fact that he was a one-armed player. Back of that fact lies a story which qualifies him plainly enough to bear henceforth the spiritual name of Barnabas. He had always played a reasonably good game of tennis with his right hand, until he was thirty-three years old. Then his right arm was shot off in a hunting accident. One can hear his friends commiserating him for the hard luck that deprived him of his tennis arm; but they did not know their man. After the accident which seemed to end his tennis career at thirty-three, he taught himself to play with his left hand, tossing up the ball for his service with the same hand that held the racquet. At forty-five he played his way through a field of sixty-four veterans, all the rest of whom were still playing as they had begun, and won the title in a stiff three-set final match. To those of us who are in the forties that achievement brings so much encouragement that Mr. Charest never needs to say anything about it at all.

Then there are men and women whose heartening deeds become habits, and grow into a kind of living that will always make us think of Barnabas as their inevitable spiritual name. All the world knows that the University of Chicago was founded in its financial resources by John D. Rockefeller, and in its educational policies and program by William R. Harper. Those who know the circumstances of its foundation, however, will always hold in honor and gratitude beside them, one who has often been called the spiritual founder of the university, Dr. Thomas W. Goodspeed. When Mr. Rockefeller offered, in 1889, to give $600,000 toward an endowment for a new university in Chicago, provided $400,000 more in good pledges were secured within the following year, Dr. Goodspeed had no illusions as to the difficulty of meeting so formidable a condition. In a personal letter at that time, commenting on the enthusiastic acceptance of the offer by the American Baptist Education Society, he wrote: "I guess I am alone in my fears, but the confidence of the brethren appalls me. It seems to me like the confidence of children, who do not consider the stupendous difference between $4 and $400,000, and lightly think it as easy to raise one sum as the other." But when his associates turned unanimously to him as the only man to take the lead in securing the $400,000, he gave himself utterly to what looked at times like an impossible task—and succeeded. Looking back in later life upon that critical year in the history of the new educational enterprise, he wrote: "I have never changed my mind as to the fearful risks we ran of failure . . . I think it was because I knew the difficulties and, having decided to face them, determined at all cost to overcome them that we finally pulled through."

Those who in later years saw him in his seventies regularly taking the lead in forward movements in both the church and the community, with the characteristic words, "Brethren, we can do this thing perfectly well"; those who knew his power as a favorite speaker at football rallies to the very end of his days, especially when the team seemed to be facing heavy odds—will none of them ever forget his contagious gift of encouragement. One of his sons recalls the first sermon he ever heard his father preach, taken from the text, "David encouraged himself in his God." That became the secret of his own success, in matters great and small alike, through a long life of leadership and achievement. Some of us will always remember him as the best example of a modern Barnabas we have ever known, one whose whole life, in word and deed alike, said to his associates in many a difficult undertaking, "Brethren, we can do this thing perfectly well."

Therein he laid hold of one of the deep secrets and mighty energies of creative religious faith in every age. There is a familiar story in the New Testament that Jesus chose among his first followers an impetuous but vacillating fisherman whose name was Simon, and so transformed him in that fellowship that afterward and ever since he has been known as Peter—the rock on whose loyalty and faith the Christian church was built. We live in other days, marked by widespread discouragement that too often deepens into disillusionment. If and when, in the company of Christ, there comes to us also a transformation in attitude and spirit like that which gave new names to at least two of his early followers, one new name that would peculiarly fit the deepest needs and help to change the too prevalent spiritual climate of our own time, would be Barnabas—Son of Encouragement.

The TRUEST TEST of RELIGION

V

Every evening, from the top of the towering Palm-Olive
Building just north of the Chicago Loop, the Lindbergh
Light swings its long finger slowly round the dark horizon;
and even the clouds in a murky sky are illuminated when
that powerful beam touches them. Just so down the generations, in the Bible and out of it, great souls in whose
minds and hearts the light of God has shone forth, have
surveyed the horizon of mystery within which our human
life is set, and with a flash of insight have lit up the obscur-
ities that puzzle and confuse the rest of us. I am asking
your attention now to one such flash of insight which we
owe to one of the most discerning minds of the last generation—William James.

In conversation some one once asked the famous psy-
chologist and philosopher for a definition of spirituality.
After some reflection James replied, "No, I'm afraid I can't
give you a good definition of spirituality; but I can point
you to a good example of a spiritually-minded man, and
that man is Phillips Brooks."

Let us follow that flash of insight now as it illuminates
successively three perplexities that puzzle our own generation. The first of these obviously has to do with the *pros*
and *cons* of definition—its indispensable values, and its
inevitable limitations. The youngest freshman in college
has been handling ideas long enough to have discovered
how necessary it is in clear and sound thinking to define
and keep defining its terms. When you take a package to
the expressman for shipment, it is important for him to
know how big it is, and how heavy, and what it contains;

and his yardstick and scales, and if necessary his gimlet, are the implements he uses to find out. Constant definitions are the scales and yardstick and gimlet of the thinking process, telling us how inclusive and how substantial are the ideas we use, and just what they contain. And definition becomes the more necessary when we undertake to ship ideas from one mind to another in discussion—as everyone finds out who tries to get anywhere with a discussion of any large subject from politics to religion. Such discussion is very much like football in the rain: every few minutes the ball has to be wiped clean and dry of muddiness and slipperiness by the reiterated question—"Now just what do you mean by that?"—else everybody will get to fumbling, and the outcome will depend more on flukes than on the merits of the question itself.

But when this indispensable importance of precise definition for all sound thinking and profitable discussion has been fully recognized, it must be recognized also that all definitions have also their own very definite limitations. The expressman's scales and yardstick and gimlet can measure very accurately the size and weight and contents of a package, for these questions are fully determined within the package itself. But if he asks how much the package is worth, other considerations which involve complicated factors of supply and demand that lie outside the package itself enter into the answer; and these subtler relationships lie beyond the reach of scales or yardstick. Even a succession of figures after a dollar sign may not be an adequate measurement of the value of the package to certain persons—as in the case of a trinket of little market value which happens to be a family heirloom, or the gift of a friend no longer living.

Just so definition is an implement of thought that is indispensable for certain purposes, but inadequate for others. Many of us find that out when we go abroad and try to use a foreign language, only to discover, sometimes to our embarrassment, how many connotations and overtones there are in the use of words which their definition in the dictionary does not and cannot tell us. A Chinese student in this country tells the delightful story of a fellow country-woman who came to America very proud of her English as she had learned it in school and from the dictionary. When she rented a house for her family, she took the wise precaution of bargaining in advance with the carpenter whom she called in to make certain minor alterations, only to find, as have Anglo-Saxons also, that the bill he later presented was considerably larger than the amount they had agreed upon for the job. Whereupon she expostulated with him in this delightful fashion, "Sir, you are very much dearer to me than when we were engaged." Her diction-ary would doubtless have sustained her use of the two critical words in that sentence in a strictly business sense, but to most of us they immediately convey certain romantic overtones of which she was utterly unaware.

And with that we have already passed over into a realm where definition is notoriously inadequate—the realm of humor. One who has ever been asked to explain the point of a joke to some one who doesn't see it, has found him-self faced with a task for which definition is the wrong tool. The humor lies in some incongruity or irony or exaggera-tion among the elements of the situation, which has to be seen in a flash of insight if it is to be seen at all. It is like a shooting star flaming for an instant across the midnight sky: you exclaim with wonder and delight if you happen to be looking that way and see it—but usually miss it if some one else has to tell you to look round and see. Ex-planations of the point after the story has been told are usually as far from bringing forth laughter as descriptions of the falling star from producing wonder and joy. What suddenly seems funny now, is no longer so much the point of the joke, as the inability of certain persons to see it. Moreover, the humor shines not from some general qualities common to a class of things defined or described in the abstract as humorous; it sparkles always in a particular situation. James might have said with equal truth that he could not give a good definition of humor; but that he could point to humorous situations, and to witty men who can recognize and even create them.

All this is no less true of beauty. Who can adequately define its nature or its secret, as it reveals itself to us in the proportions of Lichfield or Salisbury Cathedral, in the Allegretto of Beethoven's Seventh Symphony, in a sunset down the long Mediterranean, or the awful majesty of Kanchenjunga at sunrise? James might likewise have said that he could not give a good definition of beauty; but could point to things beautiful in abundance, to many folk who can recognize them at sight, and to some who can create them.

This is yet more true in the realm of human relationships. Try your own hand at a good definition of friendship or still more of love; and by so much as your own experience in these matters is deep and rich, you are likely to tear up your successive attempts as utterly inadequate. I remember from my boyhood the prize-winner in a competition for the best definition of a friend. Properly speaking, it is not a definition at all, but a picture of a man proving his friendship in a crisis—like Jesus' parable of the Good Samaritan in answer to the question "Who is my neighbor?" It ran thus: "A friend is the first person who comes in, after all the world has gone out at your door." The author of that insight would have agreed with James: he could not give a good definition of friendship, but he could point to a man who showed in a pinch that he had the mind and heart of the matter in him.

Not only the affections that transfigure human life, but the loyalties that command and the devotions that consecrate it, lie thus in large part beyond the boundaries of accurate definition, and can be expressed only in symbols.

What grateful alumnus can find words for all that *alma mater* means to him, or what patriot do justice to his fatherland with either definition or description? Dean Sperry has pointed out, with even more reason, that no genuinely religious man can ever tell all that he means when he says "God." Jesus himself continually implied as much when he never sought to define or prove God, but always spoke of him with symbols drawn from human experience at its highest and best, and then added, "How much *more* your Father in heaven." Here doubtless too is one reason why Christian thinking, when pressed for a definition or proof of the Divine, has so often said in substance what James replied to his questioner: No, we cannot give you a good definition; but we can point you to a human life, lived "by the help and under the eyes of God."

The point of all this is not at all that it is either foolish or forbidden to use definition in any or all of these fields, just so far as it will take us. As we saw at the beginning, clear thinking must always keep asking itself just what it means by the terms it uses: and religion in our own time owes too much to its thinkers who are persistently asking just what we mean when we say "God," to rest satisfied in any fog of obscurantism. The point is that there is more in all these matters than the best of definitions can fully compass. There are several questions about a violin which it is desirable and may be important to answer: how big is it, how heavy is it, what is it made of? Yardstick and scales and gimlet are the proper implements for these questions. But if we want to know what the violin can do and what, therefore, it is worth, we must bring to it another implement more closely adapted to its nature and capacities. Only a bow that can set its strings into vibration, and that bow in the hand of a master who has disciplined himself until he can draw out those capacities to the full, will tell us how good a violin it is. So in all these matters definition is the yardstick and disciplined appreciation the bow; and most of us find it a far longer and harder task to master the bow than to apply the yardstick.

So James' flash of insight falls next upon the nature of religion. It is not primarily a set of ideas, to be stated in a series of doctrinal propositions to which the rational intellect gives or withholds assent. It is more deeply an attitude toward life, a way of living, slow and difficult to learn; and best recognized and tested, therefore, in the lives of those who have mastered its secrets. Like humor, it is given ("revealed" is religion's own word) to men in flashes of insight, which reveal life itself, with all its incongruities and ironies, as something that can be trusted, and therefore adventured with confidence and expectation. Like beauty, it sees the significance of the smallest act, and of each individual life, in their organic relationship to the whole order and process of the universe. Like friendship and affection, it experiences that relationship in terms increasingly personal, whereby man knows himself to be precious in the sight of the Lord, and answers love with love. Like all devotion, it finds life fullest when it humbles itself and finally forgets itself in consecration to a Greater Purpose never fully understood, but glimpsed whenever men look up from the best they have attained to find themselves beckoned still farther forward.

Every generation of men finds it all too easy to intellectualize this way of life into a system of ideas congenial to its own forms of thought, and capable, therefore, of adequate definition within them. We modern folk find no little fault with our ancestors for thus codifying religion into theologies consonant with their geocentric view of the universe and their soul-and-body theory of man, and then handing these doctrines down to us as literal truth. But we make the same mistake when we rationalize religion into the terms of our current physics or sociology or psychology as if these in their turn were final; and a similar mistake when we assume that our favorite modern approach to religion, as a subject for "discussion" through consideration in a "discussion group," can take the place of the paths of worship and prayer, service and sacrifice, as the highroad to the discovery of God. Such religious discussion, giving natural opportunities for the raising of perplexing questions and the comparing of different points of view, is clarifying and very valuable in days of confusion like our own: but so long as religion is something more than a set of ideas calling for more exact formulation, discussion is an approach to the temple rather than an experience within its inner shrine.

It is not hard to see, therefore, why religion makes special difficulties for the characteristic mind-set of our own generation. We have become expert with yardstick, gimlet, and scales, and have developed a scientific method in their use that has made possible the amazing achievements of modern science in the analysis, measurement, and utilization of the things that are in the heavens above and in the earth beneath. But in the arts that enrich and ennoble life: the creative arts of music and poetry and painting and letters, the art of friendship and of appreciative and stimulating human intercourse, the art of living together as groups and races and nations in mutual respect and contribution and coöperation, the art in short of living happily and richly—we are, in the euphemism of the hour, "not so good." The very phrase "living well" we currently interpret not in terms of quality of life at all, but in terms of the amount and cost of things we possess and consume. Our civilization has thus become "an improved means to an unimproved end." We have produced so many things without knowing how to distribute them, that they have piled up around us until we are like to be buried beneath them, and to receive from posterity the epitaph which John Burroughs' friend proposed for his wife if he outlived her, "Died of Things."

Consequently, with all of our historical scholarship, we find it hard to understand the great religious personalities, like Gandhi in our own time, or Jesus in his. Our intellectuals, yardstick and gimlet in hand, go back across the centuries to ask what new and original ideas Jesus taught. Meanwhile the man in the street, scrambling for his share of the mounting pile of things to be possessed, in order to be sure at the end of the day that he can answer as he likes the old questions, "What shall we eat, what shall we drink, and wherewithal shall we be clothed?"—finds it very hard to understand in India now, or in Palestine then, a man who maintains that life consists not in the abundance of the things that a man or a nation or a generation possesses. But neither definition nor debate will ever do justice to the quality of his living, which was Jesus' greatest gift to mankind. He took human life as an instrument from the hand of God, and out of it drew such melody and harmony that men have listened ever since to catch the strains of his music that echo down the centuries—and they listen still whenever they hear that authentic note. No, they say with William James, we cannot give you a good definition of religion; but we can point you to one who has lived it.

And so our flash of insight falls finally on the truest test of religion in every generation: its power to produce and keep on producing such men and women. Not so much by the logical consistency of its doctrines or even the efficiency of its institutions, as by its power to lift individual lives to new levels of quality, and to bring forth in every generation the spiritual predecessors and successors of Phillips Brooks who can commend religion to their contemporaries as he commended it to James, will religion rise or fall in human regard.

Most of us know some such men and women in our part of the world, and in our own church; and some of us would add that such folk in our observation usually make this impression on others without knowing it themselves. One of the truest insights in the Old Testament is that which quaintly runs, "Moses wist not that his face shone." On the wall of Christ Church in Winnetka, one of the northern suburbs of Chicago, hangs a memorial tablet bearing this inscription: "Thanking God for the dear memory of Frederic Greeley, whose unfailing courage and kindly cheer enriched the life of this parish and made lighter the common burden." Those of us who knew him but slightly suspect that he himself would have read that sentence with amazement and incredulity. Like Moses, he wist not that his face shone.

We who spend our summers in northern latitudes have often stepped out-doors from our brightly lighted cottage after dark before the moon has risen, and in the sudden contrast from light to darkness felt at first that the night was black indeed. But as our eyes accustom themselves to the darkness around us, we make a great discovery, at first in the black heavens above us, and then in the black water beneath. Perhaps it was some such discovery that prompted Bayard Taylor to write:

> The healing of the world
> Is in its nameless saints. Each separate star
> Means nothing, but a myriad scattered stars
> Break up the night and make it beautiful.

RELIGION *as* REFUGE—*and as* CHALLENGE

VI

"Lead me to the rock that is higher than I."
Psalms LXI:2.

To anyone who has ever roughed it through Palestine in early March, a sentence like this brings back vivid memories. We of the West think of the desert as a home of heat. But the Arabs call the high plateaus of Hauran, northeast of the Sea of Galilee, "the home of the cold." And those of us who have ridden on horseback across those wind-swept plateaus, hour after hour and even day after day in the teeth of a driving northeast rain, until, chilled and weary, we seized a few moments' welcome respite in the lee of a great rock, where the sudden quiet from the piercing wind and the secure shelter from the slanting rain live yet in our grateful memories, can sense something of what must have been in the mind and heart of this poet of long ago. "Lead me to the rock that is higher than I."

Or if, later in the advancing season, one has ever sought protection from the blazing sun, and the hot blasts and stinging sand that burst from the furnace door of the desert when it is really the home of the heat; and has found that shelter at last in the only shade on earth that is at once solid and moist and cool—what Isaiah calls "the shade of a great rock in a weary land"—then one understands why the prophet used this picture to describe what the friendship of a great and good man is like. "And a man shall be as a hiding-place from the wind, and a covert from the tempest . . . as the shade of a great rock in a weary land." Still plainer is it why the Psalmist used this same picture

63

to describe his longing for the presence and the protection of God. "Lead me to the rock that is higher than I."

But just as memories like these seemed to lead to the conclusion that the main point of this text is religion's promise of secure shelter from the storm and heat of life, one's eye falls on the marginal rendering of this same familiar verse—and at once a very different picture rises before the mind's eye. "Lead me to a rock that is too high for me." The setting is no longer that of a driving storm or a burning sun, from which the unlucky traveler seeks shelter behind and beneath a great rock. The rock has become now a commanding summit which the exploring traveler is eager to climb. He wants the wider, farther view from its highest point, and he finds in its steep slopes a challenge to adventure and conquest. The rock calls out his utmost powers of exertion and endurance. If he cannot surmount it at his first attempt, he returns to seek some other path to the summit, or he develops his energies and endurance by discipline and training, till they are equal to the difficult ascent. And if the rock proves too high and hard for him to scale in his lifetime, or even for his children in theirs, it will stand there down the generations as an age-long challenge and incentive, until it also is at last surmounted. How many of the noblest vistas in human history, and the highest ranges of human capacity, come into view on the spiritual horizon when we see some steep rock rising sheer beyond us, and find at its foot a succession of courageous climbers saying, "Lead me to a rock that is too high for me."

Now the best way to understand a great utterance of religious experience like this may not be to turn the sermon into a learned piece of research, examining the linguistic grounds and approaches with an etymological microscope and a critical hammer in order to decide which of the two translations is the more accurate rendering of the Hebrew original. That may or may not prove interesting, and it may or may not prove important. The very ambiguity of the text may be significant. Certainly it reminds us of the two-sided aspect of great rocks in relation to our human experience. They are *both* a refuge from storm and heat, *and* a challenge to achievement. They shelter, and they stimulate. And in this double and almost paradoxical function they give us a true picture of the double and even more paradoxical provision of religion for human need.

In this vivid picture and swift insight of the ancient Hebrew poet there is anticipated the result of some of our best modern thinking about religion; but it is given to us, not as the result of abstract analysis or philosophic thought, but in a symbol of concrete and personal experience. Religion is at one of its poles the search for and the discovery of an assurance about man's place in the universe which gives him shelter and peace among the vicissitudes of life and keeps him from being overwhelmed by the storms that beat upon him. "Lead me to the rock that is higher than I." But at the other pole, religion is likewise the courageous and creative faith that urges man on and up to the scaling of heights that had hitherto seemed impossible; and when these at last have been attained, urges him still farther on to higher and harder summits that then for the first time appear beyond. When we modern folk analyze this second pole of religion as "the pursuit of a flying goal," and say that "man's reach exceeds his grasp," we are putting into other figures of speech the insight and impulse that led the Psalmist to cry out in answer to religion's challenge, "Lead me to a rock that is too high for me."

The same deep insight into the two-sidedness or "polarity" of religion in the profounder experience of men in every generation, appears in Professor Reinhold Niebuhr's discerning remark, in *Does Civilization Need Religion?* that man finds himself at once a child and a rebel in his world. The order of nature which his science studies has produced him and sustains him as apparently its highest

65

product; but on the other hand, his own emerging capacities and mounting standards of value will not let him rest satisfied with the order of nature as he finds it, but impel him to transform and even to transcend it. And vital religion deepens this duality and heightens this tension in his experience, by bidding him live in the world as a child in his Father's house, where he can be assured of "shelter in the time of storm"; and yet also as an irreconcilable rebel against things as they are, working and praying that the kingdoms of this world may become the kingdom of our Lord and of his Christ. Hence the inevitable tension in all profound and vital religion, and notably in historic Christianity, never fully reconciled, and relaxed only when its energies are reduced, between the kingdom of God as a present fact and as a future expectation.

Religion is by no means the only area of human experience in which such paradoxical polarities appear. Dean Sperry, in his book on *Reality in Worship*, has called our attention to a similar antithesis in the experience of George Mallory with Mount Everest. When he was telling his American audiences in 1922 why he had already participated in two attempts to climb the highest mountain in the world, and was about to undertake a third, he used words strikingly reminiscent of the marginal reading of this text: "If you cannot understand that there is something in man which responds to the challenge of this mountain and goes out to meet it, that the struggle is the struggle of life itself upward and forever upward, then you won't see why we go." "Lead me to the rock that is too high for me." And yet the same man who felt so strongly the challenge of the mountain, had a deep sense of its daunting and awesome aspect, and said just before the last ascent, on which he lost his life within six hundred feet of the summit, "We expect no mercy from Everest." If the highest of the Himalayas could thus call forth in the same heroic soul, now an ambition that stimulated him, and again an

66

awe that humbled him, need we be surprised that religion discovers the same paradox in the presence of the Eternal?

A similar duality lies close to the heart of another human experience that is fortunately far more familiar, and at its best even more profound. Every true lover knows what shelter and security there are in the companionship and affection of his beloved. There, more surely and far more warmly than in the lee of any rock, he can take refuge no matter how severe the storm without, and find an understanding and a love that become to him a manifestation and assurance of the very love of God himself. And yet every true lover knows also, not only the soul-stirring resolve to show himself worthy of such love, but also the realization that, no matter how hard he try, he can never fully earn or deserve it—indeed, that in a sense which only lovers know, his beloved is forever "beyond him." Coventry Patmore has expressed this paradox in words which many a "married lover" understands, and which strikingly recall the very imagery of the text:

> Why, having won her, do I woo? . . .
> Because her gay and lofty brows,
>   When all is won which hope can ask,
> Reflect a light of hopeless snows
>   That bright in virgin ether bask;
> Because, though free of the outer court
>   I am, this Temple keeps its shrine
> Sacred to Heaven; because, in short,
>   She's not and never can be mine.

The failure to understand and reckon with the fact of such paradoxical polarities is one cause of the inadequacy of some popular and plausible modern theories which over-confidently assume to explain these experiences—and sometimes, in the case of religion, to explain them away. It is of course true that one or the other pole of these antitheses is at any given moment in the foreground of our consciousness, and therefore dominant in our actions, just as a swinging pendulum is for the moment on one side or other of a median line. But as the movement and present position of that pendulum, even when it is swinging upward, are only to be understood, and its future direction only to be anticipated, in relation to forces that act on it, so to speak, from the other side, so the nature and value of religious experience are never exhausted by the elements that may for the moment seem to be uppermost in them.

We are often told these days, for instance, that pious people are weak souls who are always seeking shelter from the storms of life, and finding compensation for its stern realities, either in a vivid inner world of their own projection, or in hope of a happier world to come. Such an explanation moves almost exclusively within one area of religious experience, and forgets another area not less characteristic. It overlooks the tremendous energies for action which religion releases in and through men: the ancient Hebrew warrior shouting, "By thee I run upon a troop; and by my God do I leap over a wall"; and upon far loftier spiritual levels, Paul singing as he climbs higher yet, "Forgetting the things which are behind, and reaching forth unto the things which are before, I press on. . . ."

And when, on the other hand, we are told these days, with equal assurance and similar one-sidedness, that religion is simply man's own personal and social idealism unsupported by an indifferent universe, urging him onward and upward, at dusk as well as dawn, until all too soon—

> the little strength is spent
> And little hope burns low . . .

we do well to remember likewise that ancient discernment of religious aspiration, made most clearly when toward sunset the clouds lift at last from the distant heights toward which he climbs, while he himself seeks rest and shelter for yet another night: "The highest peace comes to men when their life is centered not in what is best in them, but in that beyond them which is better than their best."

This double provision of religion, affording stimulus for the day and then shelter for the night, carries with it consequences that are even more important for our living than for our thinking—just because life has to be lived before it can be understood. It has profound and immediate consequences for our *faith in God*. It is plain that both these elements were conspicuous in Jesus' faith in God—without ever being reconciled in any logical or theological definition or argument. These he apparently avoided, being content to live with and for God, and finding such life so rich and dependable that he needed no further proof. God was to him the Father out of whose strong hand neither life nor death can pluck his children. There was security now and forever. "Lead me to the rock that is higher than I." But God was also for Jesus the Incomparable Goodness, beside whom no man dare call himself good; yet whose goodness is the pattern and standard for us all. "Lead me to the rock that is too high for me." The challenge of the text rings even clearer from that supreme paradox of reverent humility and yet of limitless aspiration in the presence of God, that made Jesus say with utter sincerity: "Why callest thou me good? None is good save one, that is, God"; and yet again, "Be ye therefore perfect, even as your Father which is in heaven is perfect."

Christian thought of God and faith in God, which in Jesus swung thus from the assurance of personal security on the one hand to the sense of moral obligation on the other, has down the centuries since been always a moving pendulum, swinging in recurrent oscillation between points marked by the theological thinking, the social experience, or the religious needs of the time. The immanence and the transcendence of God, his likeness to or otherness from our human nature, the rational and the mysterious aspects of his presence in the world, and now in our own time the ethical and the cosmic elements in our conception of him, have been such theological poles, between which religious experience and thought have swung in perpetual motion and tension. And meanwhile religious men and women, whose needs have been personal and vital rather than theological, have worked their own way toward a stronger faith in God, now in a quest for deeper security and then again in response to a social or moral challenge which they had to meet—like a sailing-ship beating its way forward by tacking against the wind. So religion discovers forces that are available for quickening its own progress in situations that had looked contrary, and finds in God's will the source not only of its peace, but of its power.

This double provision of religion has consequences no less important for the Christian *view of the world*. President Hyde of Bowdoin, in a little summary of "Jesus' Way" that has been of the greatest help to many perplexed people, wrote that a Christian is one who "lives in the world as his Father's house, sharing with his brothers the good things it contains." Such joy and trustful acceptance of this world as God's world is one of religion's authentic notes, calling us to secure shelter from the storms of inner loneliness and despair that would otherwise sweep down upon our spirits. But it is by no means the only note of religion. Though this world be God's world, it is not yet fully his, nor is his will yet by any means fully done here. The house he has given us must be enlarged and transformed to fulfill his emerging purposes. The editor of *The House Beautiful* maintained in a striking editorial last summer that an old house reconstructed and improved has qualities of atmosphere and homelikeness that no new house can ever secure. So religion bids us rebuild and enlarge, not only the world and the social order of which we are a part, but our own lot in life, our own calling, our very temperament and character. Every evening God welcomes his children home to the secure shelter of a trustful faith: every morning he thrusts them forth to the challenging tasks of a creative and transforming faith.

And finally, this double provision of religion bears directly on the Christian *hope of immortality*. That faith is indeed a shelter at the last. "Lead me to the rock that is higher than I." But it is much more than a piteous cry for shelter from the storms of a pitiless universe. One of the South Side districts of Chicago has been successively represented in the state legislature by two gifted and public-spirited women, who have actually set standards for the participation of women in our political life that have measured up to the highest hopes which were so widely cherished a decade ago. Both of them died in office—all too soon. At a public memorial service for Mrs. H. W. Cheney, held in the University of Chicago chapel, Lorado Taft, the eminent sculptor, speaking for her neighbors, paid her a tribute that will not soon be forgotten. Most people, he said, depressed and weakened his own faith in immortality. But there had been a few whom he had known, Mrs. Cheney and her predecessor, Mrs. Goode, among them, who had expanded and reinforced that faith. They planned and lived life on a such a scale, made such demands on it, and cherished such great expectations beyond even the achievements that had been theirs, that he for one found his own faith in immortality renewed and enlarged as they went on before us into the Unseen. They too, he dared to believe, "asked life of Thee, and Thou gavest it."

"Lead me to the rock that is too high for me."

SPIRITUAL UNDERSTANDING

VII

"But he that received seed into the good ground, is he that heareth the word, and understandeth it."
—Matthew XIII: 23.

The greatest of all teachers of religion is describing in this familiar parable of the sower his own experiences with those he taught. He tells us frankly that he, the great master, found much of his work going for naught and bringing no result whatever; not because of any lack of vitality in the seed or of skill in the sower, but because of unfavorable conditions in the soil which he could not control. He goes on to indicate what some of these unfavorable conditions are that he found in the hearts of men, preventing religion from thriving there. Some folk, he said, have minds and hearts so hardened by continuous outside pressure, like a roadway trodden smooth and dusty by many feet, that religion never gets inside and has no real chance to grow. Some others, he found, listen eagerly and respond quickly enough, but lack that depth and tenacity of character which are as necessary to produce lasting results in religion as elsewhere in human experience. Still others, who have this disposition and mean well enough, let religion be crowded out of their lives by other interests that are less important but more insistent.

If you have ever tried to do any religious work, as a teacher in a Bible school, a church officer or visitor, a personal worker, or a preacher, you can perhaps guess what a real comfort it is to discover that Jesus himself met with the same kind of difficulties and discouragements which the rest of us find in much larger measure when we seek to

75

work in his name. But in spite of these difficulties and discouragements, he was sure that such work is tremendously worth doing, nevertheless; because, though much of it may seem not to amount to very much, some of it, falling into favorable soil, brings forth such abundant and valuable returns as to justify the whole undertaking. A wheat farmer in western Canada or the Dakotas will return to his planting after one crop failure or even more, because he knows that men must have bread to eat, and that the bounty of nature will in one good season make up for previous failures. Just so Jesus is sure that men must have the bread of life which comes down from heaven, and that in spite of failures here and there, the abundant and precious harvest in those hearts that are ready for his sowing will more than justify all work that is done in his name.

Now it is one of these difficulties, which Jesus found blocking the progress of religion in the world and in the hearts of men, that I am asking you to think about with me this morning. Matthew in his version of the parable puts a triple stress upon it. The lack of it Jesus declares to be the first great obstacle that religion meets among men: "When anyone heareth the word of the kingdom, and *understandeth* it not, then cometh the wicked one, and catcheth away that which was sown in his heart." The possession of it he later emphasizes as a main element in all good soil for religion: "But he that received seed into the good ground is he that heareth the word and *understandeth* it." Then, as if not content with these two separate emphases, he returns again to the same point at the end of the seven parables which Matthew has collected in Chapter 13, with this pointed question to his followers, "Have ye *understood* all these things?"

What now is this "understanding" which Jesus thus declares to be an indispensable condition of religious receptivity and fruitfulness? Plainly it is not a purely intellectual capacity. The man who can fully understand an exposition of Einstein's theory of relativity or of the interior structure of the atom as understood by modern physics, does not necessarily possess the spiritual understanding of which Jesus is speaking, great as may be his philosophical and scientific erudition. If we are tempted to identify this spiritual understanding with intellectual power as such, we need only remember that significant utterance of Jesus: "I thank Thee, O Father, Lord of heaven and earth, because Thou hast hid these things from the wise and prudent, and hast revealed them unto babes." Equally significant is the reminder of Paul to his Corinthian Christians: "For ye see your calling, brethren, how that not many wise men after the flesh, not many mighty, not many noble, are called: but God hath chosen the foolish things of the world to confound the wise."

It is equally plain that what Jesus means by spiritual understanding is not to be identified simply with eager listening and quick emotional responsiveness. His comparison of such natures to shallow soil, in which the seed springs up quickly, only to wither in the heat, has become a classic description of a certain kind of temperament in many other realms besides religion. We must not conclude, therefore, that those who are easily excited or quickly moved by religious appeal are necessarily those who have what Jesus means by understanding.

What he means and what we are seeking is rather something that lies in between these two extremes. It is neither mere intellectualism on the one hand, nor yet mere emotionalism on the other. Difficult as it may be to define or to describe exactly every subtle and accurate language has certain words which convey it. In our own English speech, perhaps the most adequate word is "insight." We know well enough what we mean when we say that one person has spiritual insight and another lacks it. In the original Greek of the parable itself, the verb translated "understand" means literally "to put things together." That at once suggests our common English expression "I can put two and two together." The man of spiritual understanding, in other words, is he who can "put two and two together" with instinctive accuracy in the realm of the spirit. Possibly, however, the metaphor is geometrical rather than mathematical. What Jesus was constantly doing in his parables was to put the world of nature or human society and the spiritual world side by side, and then to point out the likeness or differences between them. The man of spiritual understanding is he who can thus put the outer and inner realms together and see where they correspond. He "understands" not only the parable, but the word of the kingdom itself.

But perhaps we moderns, with our wireless and our radio, have an even more striking illustration of such spiritual understanding, in one of the familiar essentials of all communication through the invisible air. The receiving wireless station must be attuned to the sending instrument, if it is to get the message. The broadcasted music or address will be heard only by those instruments that are on the same "wave-length." The invisible air about us is doubtless at this very moment vibrant with rich music and eloquent speech broadcasted from scores of stations all over the continent: but unless our instrument is attuned to the proper wave-length we shall never hear that music or that speech. So is it likewise in the realm of the spirit. There is a certain fundamental attunedness that is indispensable to the comprehension of spiritual truth. One of our American colloquial expressions recognizes this necessity even in ordinary conversation. After explaining something, we frequently say, "Do you get me?" I have often wondered whether this very colloquial expression betrays the influence of the radio on our common speech. In any case it points to the fundamental condition of all understanding between different minds and hearts, intellectual and spiritual alike.

Perhaps the radio and the wireless may help us to understand what is, to many younger people especially, one of the most perplexing facts about religious experience; namely, that so many men and women, whom at other points we respect and admire, do not seem to possess it. Here, for instance, is a man of affairs, who understands with a quickness and accuracy that amazes us, the intricate affairs of modern business and finance. In his club or at the Stock Exchange he will listen for a moment to the ticker that is to us simply a rattle of meaningless noises, and can understand its message so quickly and surely that in the next few moments he may bring off a deal involving a large profit or avoiding a threatened loss; while we for our part are still wondering what the queer little machine is all about. That is his wave-length. Here is a woman whose familiarity with the world of social convention and relationships is so quick and intuitive that she can catch instantly the meaning of a lifted eyebrow or a shade of intonation, and is mistress of the arts of conversation and entertainment to a degree that is our admiration and perhaps our despair. That is her wave-length. But speak to this man or this woman of those ominous rumblings of social unrest and racial discontent and ambition that vibrate all around our world these days, and that seem to many of us portentous of great impending changes in our social order, and you will frequently find that this same man and woman do not "get you" any more than they hear or understand what you are talking about. Secure within the standards and habits of their own familiar world, and smug sometimes with its cocksure complacencies, they simply do not understand what to many other folk is plain to see and hear in this age of impending social change and racial readjustment.

Here again is another man to whom Einstein's theory of relativity, or the mysteries of modern physics, are familiar subjects about which he can talk fluently in a highly technical language that the rest of us cannot understand. This is his wave-length: and his quick sensitiveness and intelligence in this his world amaze and bewilder the rest of us. But when you speak either to this man of science, or that man or woman of the world, of those messages of love and goodness which God is daily sending out to those who have ears to hear; of that fellowship with Him, Whom to know aright is life eternal: then again all three alike may look blank with a sincere perplexity, and confess frankly that they do not understand. Not only in this parable, but time and again besides, did Jesus recognize what remains a frequent fact of human experience to this day; that spiritual truth is discerned and spiritual life is shared only by those whose hearts are attuned thereto. "Blessed are they that do hunger and thirst after righteousness: for they shall be filled." "Blessed are the pure in heart: for they shall see God."

But it is not simply that people outside the world of religion thus fail to understand it. One of the striking facts of Christian history has been that, not only in Jesus' own time, but through all the centuries since, so many religious leaders and workers have themselves failed to understand him. It is plain enough that this was true of the religious leaders of his own day; and it has sometimes been true of the leaders of the Christian church in other days. I wonder if the truth we are considering this morning, especially as it is illustrated by the radio, does not help us here also. We can hardly hope to understand Jesus unless our perspectives, standards, and purposes have begun to be in tune with his own.

In every generation, for instance, there are those whose wave-length in religion is that of signs and wonders. As Jesus himself said of such in his own day: "Except ye see signs and wonders, ye will not believe." It is plain enough that he was not understood then by those who were insistent on signs and wonders as the evidence of his authority and power; and one wonders whether there is not a similar warning against an overemphasis on miracle in the religious thinking of our own time.

Again, there are other folk whose religious wave-length is that of a certain familiar form of words. Unless the service of worship follows the ritual to which they are accustomed, or unless the statement of faith is expressed in their own theological creed, they can neither understand nor share in it. And when some one undertakes to state the Christian faith in terms that do not use their particular phraseology, they may not recognize it as the Christian faith at all. Happy is he whose wave-length for devotion is not limited to a single ritual, nor his wave-length for faith to a single formal creed. He will hear God speaking where others may miss him altogether, and will contribute his own part to a spiritual harmony that is richer far than any single note can ever be.

Here also we come upon a situation that in our own time has too often divided the younger and the older generation in matters religious. Older Christians are quick and sensitive of ear to that eternal message of the grace of God to the individual human soul in all its various needs, which has always been an essential part of the gospel. "Come unto Me, all ye that labour and are heavy laden, and I will give you rest." The younger generation, on the other hand, is recovering a sense for what it loves to call the "social gospel." This is as old as Amos and Hosea, John the Baptist and Jesus himself; but at some periods of its history the Christian church has lost this social wave-length from its spiritual perceptions. Too often in our own time older and younger Christians debate the social and the individual gospel as if they were alternatives. The true relationship between them is not "either . . . or," but "both . . . and." He who is to understand the fullness of the gospel of Christ for our own time must be able to "listen in" on both these wave-lengths; the will of God for the individual and for human society no less.

Some of you are already raising the profounder question: What can one do to change one's own wave-length: If we have been missing any part of the message of Jesus or the will of God for our own lives or for the life of our time, what can we do about it? The answer is partly in God's hands. When the relations between science and religion have become more clearly understood and mutually helpful than they are as yet, I have faith to believe that we shall discover new spiritual values in the old doctrine that God is our Creator. If the prophet long ago could remind himself that he was but clay in the hands of the Great Potter, surely we may put our lives, like a radio instrument in the hands of one who knows well how to adjust it, into the hands of our Maker. So may we "commit the keeping of our souls unto Him, as unto a faithful Creator."

But part of the responsibility is also our own. Every radio enthusiast knows the little handle which the listener may turn in order to adjust his instrument to different wave-lengths. As that handle is turned, there is first a buzz and a roar—and then the harmony of clear music. So Jesus has pointed out certain readjustments which we may make in our own lives, that will increase our spiritual capacity and make more sensitive our spiritual hearing. One of these is humility of spirit: "Except ye be converted, and become as little children, ye shall in no wise enter into the kingdom of heaven." Persistent eagerness of desire is another. "Ask, and it shall be given you; seek, and ye shall find; knock, and it shall be opened unto you." The third and most effective is a daily determination to do the will of God as He shall make it known. "Not every one that saith unto me, Lord, Lord . . . but he that doeth the will of my Father Who is in heaven." "If any man will do his will, he shall know."

REFINING RELIGION

VIII

The highest authorities in matters religious tell us that we get ahead much farther and faster in religion with the aid of symbols, illustrations, analogies—always provided they are true analogies—than by the use of abstract statements such as definitions and creeds. The parables of Jesus are, of course, the supreme example of insight and artistry in such use of analogy. "The Kingdom of heaven is *like* . . ." It is striking to find that much of our best recent thinking in religion, particularly on the urgent contemporary problem of its relation to science, as represented by Whitehead of Harvard, Wieman of Chicago, and even more explicitly by Streeter of Oxford in his notable recent book *Reality*, emphasizes the close kinship of religion in such use of symbols to poetry, art, and even humor. Religion and science are like our right and left hands: two implements for getting at and handling reality from different sides, relatively independent and decidedly different—as we find quickly enough when we try to put the same glove on each hand; each, however, helping the other, and both together able to accomplish much more than either one alone.

It is one of the encouraging signs of contemporary progress in religious thought and life, that religion is finding so many of its most helpful analogies and symbols in other realms, and not least in the realm of science itself. Who of us has not heard the radio and the wireless recently used to illustrate some age-long truth about prayer, or spiritual-mindedness? I am taking to guide our thought today another such analogy, which I frankly and gratefully owe to Dean Inge, that extraordinary Englishman whose originality and penetration are always stimulating, even when one cannot wholly agree with him. Religion, he says, is like certain chemical elements which are not found in nature pure, but only in combination with other elements. You who are working in chemistry will at once think of several such, but we all are familiar with iron as an everyday illustration of this point. Iron is given to us in nature only as ore: and between that ore and the iron and steel which support our civilization there is always somewhere a furnace.

Just so is religion in human history and experience. We never find it absolutely pure, but always in combination with elements less worthy, less permanent, less winsome. It turns up all too frequently in combination with ideas which intelligent folk can no longer accept, or with institutions which progressive folk can no longer approve: but that does not mean that the religious elements in the combination are invalid or unimportant even though these theological or ecclesiastic elements may be long since outgrown. So, too, we find religion constantly embodied in personalities, many of whose characteristics do not appeal to us at all; whose narrowness, or rigidity, or complacency, or fanaticism may indeed strongly repel us. Some searching modern wit has observed that the trouble with our world is that the godly are so inhuman, and the human are so ungodly! Even more delightful is the remark of another contemporary that city churches are composed of a great many people who don't know one another, and wish they did; while country churches are made up of a few people who do know one another, and wish they didn't! Fair and accurate discrimination between the personal and social values of religion as it is actually given to us in the people that we know, and the obvious limitations of their own personalities, is all too rare in our modern evaluations of religion. The iron is too frequently discarded because the ore seems difficult to work.

This is true not only of ordinary folk like ourselves, but even of the greatest figures in religious history and experience. Many of us would doubtless agree that Mahatma Gandhi is the outstanding religious figure of our own generation: but one of the most puzzling facts about his enigmatic personality is the combination in him of so much of the beauty, serenity, and dynamic power of vital religion, with certain economic and scientific ideas and political programs that seem to us Occidentals naïve, if not childish. Even of him whom we Christians recognize as religion's incomparable incarnation and God's clearest revelation in all human history, does this same principle hold to a degree that constantly perplexes us when we try to copy him most closely. His life was set in an Oriental environment, and expressed itself in certain ancient forms of thought and action, which we Western moderns cannot repeat or imitate without unreality; and his personality possessed a uniqueness whose most admirable and lovable qualities seem hopelessly beyond our personal attainment. More and more clearly we are realizing that to follow him in the twentieth century means, not to copy slavishly his outward manner of life or forms of thought, but rather to catch his spirit and attitudes, and embody them again in a modern translation into the terms of our own day and generation.

This situation and this necessity are by no means peculiar to religion. Josiah Royce, in his *Spirit of Modern Philosophy*, makes this significant comment on the life and thought of the ancient Greeks:

And now perhaps you may already see why there is of necessity nothing absolute, nothing final, about much that a Plato himself may have looked upon as absolute and as final in his work. Greek life was not all of human life; Greek life was doomed to pass away; Greek instincts and limitations could not be eternal. The crystal heavens that the Greek saw above him were indeed doomed to be rolled up like a scroll, and the elements of his life were certain to pass away in fervent heat.

But then, into all nobler future humanity Greek life was certain to enter, as a factor, as a part of its civilized instincts, as an ennobling passion in its artistic production, as a monument of its spirituality. . . .

With the life whose temperament it reflectively embodied the philosophy will pass away. It will pass away, but it will not be lost. A future humanity will, if civilization healthily progresses, inherit the old kingdom, and reëmbody the truly essential and immortal soul of its old life. This new humanity, including in itself the spirit of the old, will need something, at least, of the old philosophy to express in reflective fashion its own attitude toward the universe. This something that it needs of the old philosophy may not be that which the philosopher had himself imagined to be his most absolute possession. Like the statesman, he will have builded better than he knew. . . .

No, the philosopher's work is not lost when, in one sense, his system seems to have been refuted by death, and when time seems to have scattered to scorn the words of his dust-filled mouth. His immediate end may have been unattained; but thousands of years may not be long enough to develop for humanity the full significance of his reflective thought.

The principle thus clearly stated by the great modern philosopher comes to even more vivid utterance in a sentence of Paul written to the Corinthians, which is my text today, "We have this treasure in earthen vessels" (II Cor. 4:7). The priceless jewel of religious faith is constantly given to us in some earthen container whose value is altogether incommensurable with that of the treasure which it contains. These earthen vessels are time and again broken or outworn; but that does not invalidate the worth of the contents, or lessen the loss if in the breaking of the vessel the jewel disappear. In periods of rapid religious transition and changing forms of thought like our own, when the air is full of the dust of breaking earthenware and the ground is covered with its fragments, it is all too easy for treasures of inestimable value to be lost amid the inevitable confusion

88

that results. He is the wise man in such a situation who seeks for and holds to the jewels at whatever cost, realizing that the earthen vessels must perish with the using, but that the treasures they contain may keep and even increase their value down the generations.

This principle is of the greatest importance for the discriminating study of religion in human history. The student of primitive ideas or institutions, and of all ancient civilizations, is constantly finding religion mixed up with superstitions which he cannot accept, and engines of social repression or exploitation which he cannot approve. The mixture seems in many cases such low-grade ore that he is often inclined to reject it altogether as not worth working— except, perhaps, as a purely historical phenomenon. Meanwhile, however, there may be in the mixture certain values of social discipline and coöperation, and certain spiritual convictions of personal responsibility to a higher power, that we moderns must not overlook or underestimate, simply because we do not need or want either medicine-man or priest. To one who is acquainted with the wealth of the Mesaba Range in high-grade iron ore, and the modern processes of iron- and steel-making, the iron mines long since abandoned that Greece and Rome once used may well seem negligible, if not indeed pathetic; but that sense on our part does not mean that they were not very much worth working in their own day, or that our own civilization would have been possible if they had not then been worked by long generations of men who found them indispensable for their own age, and out of them laid the foundations of our own civilization.

This is true of much higher stages of religion as well. Reading the Psalms, I have found myself more than once a bit put off by what struck me at first as the rather smug and self-centered appeal of the consciously righteous man to Jehovah for personal prosperity and protection against his enemies. Then suddenly I realized that here for the first time in religious history the spiritual experience and personal values of the *individual*, as over against the pressure of society and the apparent inexorability of fate, were struggling for recognition and utterance. That inner conviction of the individual's infinite significance, that confident appeal to God and the future for personal approval and support, is one of the priceless treasures of human experience and one of the indispensable elements in human progress. The quartz rock in which it is imbedded may feel to us moderns at first rather angular and hard; but it is gold-bearing quartz, and runs high!

This is especially true of much mediæval religion, the superstitions and other-worldliness of which we enlightened moderns are accustomed to look down upon with complacent superiority. We have to admit, however, that mediæval religion supplied an energy for great adventures and achievements, and supported flights of creative imagination in all the fine arts, which we can only frankly copy when we build our churches, and must purchase at enormous cost when we equip our art museums. Crude oil as it comes from the earth may not look or smell attractive to our modern taste; but it contains within itself the energies which drive our automobiles and support our airplanes. The modern man's frequent sense of superiority to all religion may yet prove to be as shortsighted and impoverishing as would be his refusal to have anything to do with crude oil.

All this is hardly less true of certain forms of contemporary religion which as educated men we find it difficult to approve. Cruising along the Maine coast and finding ourselves fog and storm bound over Sunday in a fishing village far from the railroad, a college mate and I hunted up a little Baptist church where our small party constituted one-fifth of the entire congregation. The preacher was a dear old man, vigorously fundamentalist in his theology, who in the midst of a sermon on love to Jesus suddenly seemed to forget his subject in the heat of his denunciation of city churches and ministers, whose theological thinking and practical programs he alike disapproved—and whose present-day problems he did not in the least comprehend. As we prepared our evening meal aboard ship under a clearing sunset sky, my college mate pointed out that we should estimate the value of that church and its type of religion altogether too cheaply if we looked simply at the theology of the preacher and condemned it all because of certain ideas of his which we ourselves could not accept. He reminded us that the truer evidences and tests of the value of religion to that community were to be found in such personalities as that of the leading man in the church, the proprietor of the local grocery store, whom we had heard speak in the service and had afterward met; a man whose face and bearing I shall never forget for their beautiful mingling of shrewdness, serenity, and strength. Being himself a city man and a suburban church leader, my college mate further remarked that we had seen in this layman a type of Christian character, growing in its own native soil and atmosphere, which our great city churches, with all their liberal theology and up-to-date methods, do not, in his judgment, any too often produce. For the truest test of religion is never the theology of its preachers, but the characters of its laymen.

The attitude, so widespread today among educated folk, which sniffs at religion as so much crude oil, points to the superstitions and exploitations and fanaticisms with which too often it has obviously been found in combination, and prefers to let the whole sticky and disagreeable mess alone, is an attitude intelligible enough—but is it an intelligent attitude? Certainly it is not the attitude that has given us the internal-combustion engine, the automobile, and now the airplane. These have been made possible by the more and more perfect refining of that same crude oil, and by the utilization of the tremendous energies which it contains for lighting and driving our modern civilization. A similar discrimination and purification are no less necessary in all matters social and spiritual. Wise men and women do not refuse to love because they do not approve of jealousy or lust; nor yet to cultivate a strong will, because they do not like stubbornness; nor yet to be ambitious, because they do not want to be selfish. All the great energies and experiences of human life lie perilously close to similar perversions or distortions. It is the task of intelligent individuals, and of a progressive generation, to perfect its spiritual chemistry until it can refine away the crudities and yet keep the energies that are contained in vital religion. Our modern age sorely needs a dynamic adequate to its social tasks, and powerful enough to overcome the spiritual inertia of the disillusionment and cynicism that never get out of the mud or off the ground. That social and spiritual energy is contained in the Christian religion; and our present task is to liberate it from ignorance, fanaticism, and superstition, and to put it to work at the great tasks that lie before our generation and our world.

This principle has an important bearing on all our religious thinking. It reminds us that vital religion may and does exist and persist in combination with theological ideas that may at the same time be changing fast and far. You who are students are highly likely, like so many of your predecessors, to find your ideas about religion undergoing some changes that may seem to you radical during your student days. As some of us look back across the years at the naïve and childish ideas about religion with which we entered college as freshmen, we rejoice now that this same thing happened to us—painful as the process of refinement certainly was at the time; for the religion that commands our allegiance now is a far clearer thing before our minds, and has far more power within our wills, than the traditional orthodoxy in which we were brought up. Nor has this refining process been confined to our undergraduate days. Are there not many of us who have found our religious symbols—the pictures at the back of our minds not only when we think, but even when we worship and when we pray—changing fast and far during these last years? Every one of us—both the sophomore, who is all upset about religion, and the professor, who is rethinking it and glimpsing dimly ahead "new thoughts of God"—is likely to feel for the moment, in the heat and confusion of the refining process, that he has lost religion and can never find it again. That does not by any means follow; what we have lost may be only some of the crudities that once went along with our religion, but need persist no longer.

Involved in all this is an implication very important to remember in any community like this one. Whether we are students or teachers, we are human enough to be in danger of supposing that vital religion only goes along with theological ideas or ecclesiastical practices just like our own. But in a community like this we are certain to find men and women whose ideas and habits in these matters are widely different from ours. The principle we are considering is the real guardian of the spirit of tolerance and comprehensiveness. Vital religion can and does thrive in combination with widely different theological ideas and ecclesiastical connections. "Judge not, that ye be not judged. . . ."

> The evening star that softly sheds
>   Its tender light on me,
> Hath other place in the heavenly blue,
>   Than that I seem to see.
> Too faint and slender is that beam
>   To keep its pathway true
> In the vast space of cloud and mist
>   It seeks an exit through.
>
> Nor light of star nor truth of God
>   To earth-born clouds and doubt

Can straightway pierce the hearts of men
    And drive the darkness out.
On bent, misshapen lines of faith
    We backward strive to trace
The love and glory that we ne'er
    Could look on face to face.

Each fails through dim and wandering sight
    The vision whole to see;
But none are there so poor and blind
    But catch some glimpse of Thee—
Some knowledge of the better way
    And of that life divine
Of which our yearning hope is both
    The prophecy and sign.

But all these problems, for our thinking and our action alike, are only to be solved as we succeed in working out the relation of religion to our own personal living. It is a fact long since discovered about the chemistry of religion that the element with which it most perfectly and powerfully leaps into combination is not an orthodox creed, nor yet an ecclesiastical institution, but rather a human life. That was the point of these closing sentences in a recent address of President Hopkins at Dartmouth that has echoed across the country:

In spite of the dangers of generalization, I, with deliberation, make this one. If the only options available to this college were to graduate men of the highest brilliance intellectually, without interest in the welfare of mankind at large, or to graduate men of less mental competence, possessed of aspirations which we call spiritual and motives which we call good, I would choose for Dartmouth College the latter alternative. And in doing so, I should be confident that this College would create the greater values and render the more essential service to the civilization whose handmaid it is.

This is even more sharply the point of the Christian religion, which finds its clearest revelation of the meaning

94

of human life, and of the character and purpose of God Himself, not in a creed or a book or an institution, but in a *person*: in the life of Jesus. And that central truth of Christianity is being constantly restated for us, as indeed it constantly needs to be, in our contemporary experience. The West Point delegation to the Northfield Student Conference was holding its delegation meeting in a dimly lighted tent some years ago, considering the bearing of the day's discussion on the problems of the West Point campus. Some one had suggested that Christianity had something to contribute to these problems, when from a dark corner of the tent came the familiar question of a perplexed generation, "What is Christianity, anyway?" There was a moment's silence, and then from another corner came an inspired answer: "Christianity? Why, Christianity is *Oscar Westover*."

How one would like to have known him—a West Point cadet whose life had so commended his religion to his mates that in his absence *he* should be offered by one of them, and accepted by the rest, as a working definition, because a living embodiment, of the essence of the Christian religion. How one wishes one knew what happened to him in the Great War—for our generation sorely needs such men as he. He cannot be copied on other campuses, by so much as West Point is different from other colleges, and his life therefore from ours. But when that difference is recognized, does it not remain true that the greatest religious need of every college campus, and indeed of every generation, is for more Oscar Westovers, among students and faculty alike? But if and when they are given to us, they will not be called Oscar Westovers: every one of them will bear his own name.

A MEMORIAL ADDRESS for
JULIUS ROSENWALD

IX

No one can review the hundreds of tributes to Julius
Rosenwald that have appeared all over the land during the
weeks since his death, without seeing at once that there is
very much more in them and beneath them than the
familiar glorification of one more self-made multimillion-
aire. Many Americans, a fair share of them Chicagoans,
have amassed great wealth in their own lifetimes; and not
so long ago Mr. Rosenwald himself was reputed to be our
wealthiest Chicagoan. But we certainly should not be holding this memorial service here in the university chapel
today, nor would these editorial and other tributes have
been written, if this were all. Nor were they written simply
because he was an open-handed and large-hearted dispenser
of his wealth. Many a gold-miner who once struck it rich,
many a successful boxer or ball-player who has been a good
fellow and an easy mark, has done that. And conspicuously
successful men have sometimes been known to cultivate
a reputation for philanthropy—like the delightful Scotch-
man who announced that he was putting into his will a
generous bequest to the widow of the Unknown Soldier!

But here was a man who in terms of quantity alone gave
away during his own lifetime four times as much money as
he left to his heirs. More important still, here was a man
whose whole career, alike as merchant, citizen, and philanthropist, was so directed and dominated by the combination
of his outstanding personal qualities that his ideas and his
attitudes have become not less influential in the life of his
generation than his great benefactions. His giving and his
living were so thoroughly of a piece that his philanthropies
projected and multiplied even to the ends of the earth what

we can now recognize as the rarest and finest qualities in the man himself. So it is not enough to celebrate any one aspect or activity of his career alone: the successful merchant, the generous philanthropist, the good citizen, the beloved neighbor and friend. We must celebrate the whole man who was all these at once—and more. Some men, said Emerson, serve their day and generation by what they do, and some by what they are. Julius Rosenwald did both. No wonder so many reckoned him the first citizen of Chicago.

This university has special reason to recognize all this. She commemorates today not only one of her most generous donors, from whose hand and heart came the geology building that bears his name, the new dormitories for men to which his gifts in money and thought were so substantial—and not least that special fund which for years has been a godsend to the university in its flexibility and availability for all kinds of urgent needs. The total of these gifts in terms of money has been over $5,000,000. The university commemorates even more a trustee who has given her twenty years of wise counsel and personal devotion that are beyond any price to purchase or estimate; who gave himself with his gifts, as he always did. She commemorates a neighbor and friend who combined in himself the qualities that this university values most, because they enlarge knowledge and enrich human life. We devote this public service of worship in the university chapel to his memory, partly because Julius Rosenwald would have been the first, modest man that he always was, to protest against our gathering together just to praise him; and still more because the true instinct of religion is always in such a case to thank God for the gift of such a man, and to pray that others like-minded and like-hearted may be raised up in his stead.

Three qualities in Julius Rosenwald stood out clearly in his relations with all great public enterprises. The first was

18679

his intelligence. A former member of our own faculty, after years of close association with him, said that he had the quickest insight and best judgment in practical affairs that he himself had ever seen. That native gift, sharpened by long experience, built up through thirty-five years a business that sends its publications to 40,000,000 people, and sold $347,000,000 worth of goods in the year 1931. That same far-sighted intelligence he then devoted through the last twenty years of his life to the giving away of over $70,000,000. By his characteristic combination of clear thinking with consistent practice, as set forth in his two well-known articles in the *Atlantic*, entitled "Principles of Public Giving" and "The Trend Away from Perpetuities," and as exemplified in the creation of his own Rosenwald Fund, he has turned the direction of large-scale public giving in America away from perpetuities toward a greater faith in living boards of trustees, and in future generations as entirely competent to carry forward under changing conditions whatever of our present philanthropic purposes may prove worthy of perpetuation. As a New York financier put it in commenting on his *Atlantic* articles, "You have made it clear that excellent intention is only part of a perfect gift and that it is possible for the best-intended public giving to result in harm instead of benefit."

He used his favorite instrument of conditional giving to arouse not only individuals, but communities and sections as well, to the more adequate meeting of their own social responsibilities. Twenty-five cities in America now have Y. M. C. A. buildings for colored youth and four cities such Y. W. C. A. buildings, toward each one of which he has given $25,000 on condition that the community itself raise $125,000. All over the South (less than one hundred counties are now without one) there are Rosenwald schools for colored children, some 4,200 in number, costing in all over $20,000,000. Of this total Mr. Rosenwald has given about $3,500,000, the negroes $4,000,000, the whites

$1,000,000, and the public tax funds $12,000,000. The leverage of these schools on the standards of education for white people in these communities has been hardly less powerful than for colored children. No wonder Miss Jane Addams said of him in 1912, long before his wisdom as a giver became world famous, "He has such a comprehensive, practical knowledge of the conditions . . . that every dollar he gives does its full value . . . there are few philanthropists who study conditions so thoroughly and practically. He has given intelligently and discriminately, always displaying the great big heart he possesses to help mankind."

With this last insight Miss Addams indicated a second outstanding characteristic of Julius Rosenwald, for which we might use either her own womanly phrase, "a great big heart," or Dr. George E. Vincent's more recent characterization, "a quite extraordinary sense of social responsibility." This quality has long been evident in his conduct of his own business. As we were standing by the window in Mr. Rosenwald's own office the other day, one of his close associates told of his solicitude from the earliest days of the company, not only for the physical surroundings and appearance of the plant, but even more for the social standards and human welfare of their employees. Then he showed me the pamphlet describing the "Employes' Savings and Profit-sharing Pension Fund," as it has been in effect since 1916. Into this fund employees may put 5 per cent of their salaries, while the company for its part puts in 7½ per cent of its net profits. Not less significant than these carefully planned welfare programs is the story recently told in the *New York Times* about the question put to him by a caller at his office late one afternoon, as 13,000 employees were pouring out of the plant. "Mr. Rosenwald, how does it feel to have so many people working for you?" "I never thought of it that way," came the quick answer; "I consider they are working *with* me."

This same sense of social responsibility appeared in all

his relationships as a citizen. Some years ago I chanced to be a member of a party returning with him from Tuskegee to Chicago on the morning after an unusually critical election. The main result of that election was a bitter disappointment to almost everyone in the group, and especially to Mr. Rosenwald himself. As we were riding in his car from the station through the familiar South Side streets, his resilient spirits rose much faster than ours from the common despondency. Presently he broke the general silence with the remark that even if Chicago did not choose its officials wisely according to his way of thinking, he could not help loving the city with his whole heart—its streets and buildings only less than its people—because it was the city whose life he himself had deeply shared for so many years. That sentence, on that morning, revealed the very soul of the man.

Even more clearly did this characteristic appear in his unique personal relationship to that tense and difficult problem of our race-conscious age and country—the problem of racial prejudice and friction. One of our own faculty who is especially conversant with this problem the world around, recently remarked that the only quality of mind and heart which can leap across the widening gulfs of race in our modern world, and build bridges of understanding across them, is imaginative and sympathetic goodwill. That was the bridge on which Juluis Rosenwald so easily and unostentatiously crossed and recrossed from one racial or religious group to another. The day of his death our own colored maid said to me that her race had lost its best friend. Almost any Christian or any Jew who has thought much on these sensitive and difficult matters will agree that Julius Rosenwald has done more than any other man of his generation to commend his own race and faith to other races, and to ease the relations between them—not so much by what he has said, as by what he has been and has done. Is it not an extraordinary fact that this one man has been the strongest personal bond in his generation, *both ways*, between the three races that find it hardest to live and work and play together in modern American life without friction?

On the banks of the Missouri River near Sioux City, Iowa, there is a region where three states come very close together: Iowa, South Dakota, and Nebraska. From a single hill-top in one state, one can look across the narrow stream into two other states. The life of Julius Rosenwald was such a point of outlook and vision. Around him three races of men came close together. He, and we when we stood with him, could see beyond the differences that divide us into the experience of races other than our own, and could recognize clearly there the familiar characteristics common to all human kind.

What were the secrets of this exceptional quality in him? Story after story could be told that would reveal some of them—and it is striking to see how many of them show the influence over him of Abraham Lincoln, in whose home city of Springfield he had himself grown up, and who from his boyhood was always his hero. The magnanimity which was one of Lincoln's rarest qualities, and which so many other American leaders have almost wholly lacked, made Julius Rosenwald slow to resent a slight, and quick to avoid giving one. I shall never forget his quiet comment, made in my hearing to some younger men who were complaining of racial discrimination, to the effect that he had never believed that it was either wise or profitable to pay too much attention to such matters. One of our own faculty tells of walking with him when they met upon the street a colleague whom Mr. Rosenwald did not at first recognize—but he at once insisted on going back to greet him when he learned his name, lest the professor should think that the trustee had forgotten or failed to consider important the fact of their having met previously.

Another such secret was the modesty that bulked so

large in his frequent insistence that business success is 95
per cent luck and 5 per cent ability, and wealth a double
accident—once in getting it, and again in keeping it. His
quiet humor was still another secret in his gift of human
understanding—delightfully illustrated in the cablegram
which he once sent from Jerusalem to Tuskegee, quoting
simply the title of one of his favorite spirituals, "I'm walking into Jerusalem just like John." And he always had a
quick sense for the universal human elements in any
sensitive situation, that led him beneath all secondary differences to the deeper levels where men meet at their best.
When a distinguished Southern scholar once said to him
in my hearing that he counted him one of the best Christians he knew, Mr. Rosenwald's quick reply was that he
could answer best in the words of Lessing's "Nathan der
Weise," that the qualities which seemed to his Christian
friend to show him a good Christian, were those which he
himself should regard as showing him to be a good Jew.

Greatest among the qualities that for some of us will
always be associated with his name, is that which our own
Professor James Weber Linn, in the most discerning tribute
which has fallen under my eye, described as Julius Rosenwald's most unique and precious spiritual possession—his
hopeful faith in the capacities and possibilities of ordinary
human beings of every race. He ascribed this faith in large
measure to the influence of Abraham Lincoln on Mr.
Rosenwald in his early years and indeed throughout his
life. There is always a genuinely religious quality about
such faith: it can never be fully demonstrated, is therefore
always open to question or doubt, and, like every ultimate
faith, calls ever for venture in the face of risk. Such was
the faith of Julius Rosenwald; he risked his money and
he spent his life for this adventurous confidence in the
capacities of common folk.

The Jewish race has steadily produced through its long
history at least three types of genius: business shrewdness

and skill, ethical and social insight, religious sensitiveness and faith. Under modern conditions these three racial gifts tend to separate, and frequently fall apart. In Julius Rosenwald all three were combined. Therein lay the measure of his greatness.

My own contacts with him brought me varied evidences of the reality and power of his religious sense. Our university board of trustees has a tradition that its meetings shall open with prayer. It is not easy to keep such a tradition from becoming a mere formality. During the ten years of my own membership on the board, no one of its members was more interested or more helpful in preventing that, or more evidently sympathetic with that part of the proceedings, than was Julius Rosenwald.

Far more significant, however, than his participation in any outward form of religious expression, was his genuinely religious attitude toward giving. One of our foremost contemporary thinkers has described religion as "being in love with loving." Julius Rosenwald was in love with giving. Giving, he said once, is "the one pleasure that never wears out." It was a joy that he loved to share with others. Shortly before we sailed for India on the Barrows lectureship, he sent me a note in his own hand, enclosing a very generous check, and saying that he was sure I would find in India many good causes to which I would like to make some contribution, and that he wanted me to have that joy and so share it with him.

Here, one suspects, lay one of the deepest satisfactions of his own life. At the dedication some years ago of a new Rosenwald school in a country district a few miles from Tuskegee, a few of his Chicago friends were present with him, together with a large company of colored people in colorful costumes from all the region round. His neighbors in Chicago know how reluctant he always was to speak in public: but that day, in an informal talk to that company of friends, colored and white, the very heart of him revealed itself. He said that he had gotten more satisfaction and joy out of his own share in making possible such schools as that one, than out of any or all of the other interests in which through a long and active lifetime he had engaged. Like another great soul of his own race and faith who lived centuries ago, he had discovered in his own personal experience that it *is* more blessed to give than to receive.

The LIFE BEYOND

X

One Easter afternoon some years ago a university professor said to me: "I'm very much of a liberal in matters religious. But once a year at least, on Easter morning, I do go to church. And I always come away unsatisfied if what we have heard is just another balancing of the old arguments, when what I'm wanting and needing is some fresh sense of newness of life."

He had put into frank and simple terms the characteristic approach of the religious man, and the distinctive contribution of religion, to the oldest question in the world: "If a man die, shall he live again?" It is a question on which it is not easy to get beyond mere balancing of arguments: as an issue for debate this always has been, and doubtless always will be, an open question. All the appearances are certainly on one side: but on the other side is the cautioning reminder of modern science, from its early days under Copernicus and Galileo to these latest days of Eddington and the new physics, that appearances are often deceitful and never final. There are plenty of arguments on both sides, and no conclusive demonstration either way; for faith in immortality, like faith in the existence and still more in the goodness of God, moves in a realm where decisive proof and disproof are alike impossible.

So, too, seem at first sight the traditional contributions of religion, and especially of the Christian religion, to this old debate. What shall we moderns make of the New Testament accounts of the first Easter—the familiar story of the empty grave, and of the appearances of the risen Christ to his disciples? Here begins another long debate, for the same evidence that seems entirely conclusive to some among us is unconvincing to others. What the former regard as a demonstration has become for the latter a part of the problem itself, adding thus new areas and complications to the old debate.

At this point, therefore, it becomes necessary to clear our minds first of all as to what it is that we may expect from religion in all these ultimate questions where debate continues down the generations, and conclusive demonstration seems to our generation more than ever impossible. Thoreau said once, with profound insight: "It is morning when it is dawn in your soul." Religion brings the dawn of a new day to the soul of man—the rising within him of a new kind and quality of life that he experiences as coming from beyond and above himself, quickening within and around him a faith and hope and love that lighten both his burdens and his perplexities, and enable him to pass even through the valley of the shadow of death, unfearing and expectant of another and brighter dawn. In the classic phrases of the Bible, the rising of the sun of righteousness brings life and immortality to light, and shineth more and more unto the perfect day. The contribution of religion to faith in immortality is therefore not so much new arguments for a debate as new experiences and a new assurance in living the kind of life that deserves to continue beyond this short and shifting mortal span.

These experiences and this assurance, however, are not given to most of us as a fixed and inalienable possession. Like the sunshine once more, they are profoundly affected by all the clouds and storms that sweep across our spiritual sky; they pass through many a night of doubt and sorrow, when the immortal hope burns low or dips beyond our horizon in some long arctic darkness. There are times in personal experience—perhaps there are even periods in human history—when religious men have to dig in and wait long for the return of the sun, like Byrd and his mates through their Antarctic winter at Little America.

It should be pointed out, too, that this assurance comes

first to many of us, like our first experience of religion itself, not so much as an achievement of our own, but rather through contact with some other person whose character or quality of life calls forth this conviction within us, as the sun calls forth life upon the earth. Faith in immortality, that is, is a claim that we make on behalf of some other people much earlier and much more strongly than we venture to make it for ourselves. This fact has an important bearing on the charge so often made of late, that belief in immortality is an egregious case of wishful thinking, a projection beyond the grave of the elemental will to live, of the instinct of self-preservation. While it may, indeed, be so in some cruder cases, the nobler and deeper faith in immortality has more often been the conviction that some other person, honored or beloved, is too worthful to perish with the body in a universe that has produced and sustained moral values and spiritual capacities like these. Faith in immortality is thus a correlative, or rather a consequence, of faith in God.

It is natural, therefore, that the great personalities of our own and of other days—especially those whose greatness has been moral and spiritual—should become not only centers, but strong supports for this faith. The New Testament abounds in evidence that this was true of Jesus to a very exceptional degree. The Book of Acts reports Peter as using in his first public address, on the Day of Pentecost, a striking phrase of which Professor Goodspeed in his American Translation has given us a highly significant rendering: "Death could not control him." It is a revealing insight that lays bare with singular accuracy some of the main roots of a living faith in immortality then and now.

One of these is its plain disclosure of the motives and the perspectives that dominated Jesus' own living. Death could not control his *actions*. He himself once put his own attitude into words that have echoed down the centuries: "Be not afraid of them that kill the body, but are not able to kill the soul: but rather fear him who is able to destroy both soul and body." And when his own life was threatened and finally taken from him, he turned his own counsel into a steadfast assurance and expectancy that dominated both his life and his death. This life was for him a room opening out into another and larger room, and death was the door leading through and beyond.

In sharp contrast with this attitude and perspective there stands another, for which death is the decisive and controlling fact about human life. Not its high capacities and possibilities, which Jesus took as central for his estimate of human destiny, but rather its brevity and mortality, give us on this view the true clue to its significance. This attitude has always been with us down the centuries; but in our own disillusioned time it has become more than ever explicit and thoroughgoing. Man, says a modern novelist, is "only a bundle of cellular matter upon its way to become manure." "Ours is a lost cause," writes a modern essayist, "and there is no place for us in the natural universe." And a modern philosopher has painted in somber colors the ultimate shadow that from his viewpoint lies inexorably across all our human scene: "Brief and powerless is man's life; on him and all his race the slow, sure doom falls pitiless and dark." These are attitudes toward life which death obviously can and does control: no wonder they have been named "futilitarian."

Most modern men, of course, are not quite so explicitly hopeless. The more prevalent attitude in these matters does not thus magnify the fact and meaning of death, but rather ignores and tries to forget it. If death, as we often complain, was much overemphasized by our great-grandfathers in their theology and our great-grandmothers on their samplers, we their descendants have certainly swung to the opposite extreme. We have left their gruesome skulls and crossbones and their solemn *memento mori* out of everything from our tombstones to our ethics and our expectations; we have shortened their long funeral services to a minimum consistent with decency, have covered the raw edges of our open graves with banks of hothouse flowers, and have turned our faces the other way as soon as our hearts will let us. Death does not control us, largely because we do not face up to it.

Jesus' attitude contrasts sharply with both of these. Unlike most of us, he had faced up both to the fact and the imminent prospect of death. Unlike our modern Futilitarians, he had found in life itself something worthful enough and powerful enough to overcome it. "Death could not control him." And down through the centuries he has quickened in countless hearts a courage and faith in the face of death like to his own. Death could not control *them*.

Thirty years ago the visiting preacher at an eastern university took as his text one Sunday morning, "I am the door." He pictured life as a series of rooms leading one into the other: home to school, school to college, college out into active life; each room a preparation for the next. What then of life itself? His closing words no hearer could easily forget. Life itself, he said, seems to bring us at last only to a blank wall. But there stands One saying down the generations, "I am the door."

Twenty-five years later that same preacher's younger son had become one of the foremost medical scientists of his generation. In the mid-forties he was stricken with inoperable cancer, and his colleagues gave him six months to live. For eighteen months he looked death in the face with level eyes; and one of his medical associates has put into memorable words an experience shared during those months by many of his friends:

The proof of a man's life—how much has been the living of a formula and how much an inward light—may often be found in the manner of his facing death. For courage is still, as it has always been, a thing of great beauty, that springs, whatever its form and expression, from an inner source of moral power. We wish, for ourselves and the ordinary human being, a swift and merciful death, which is most easily supported with dignity and composure. For him we would not have had it other than it came. Those who were fortunate in seeing him during those eighteen months when he and death sat face to face— who dreaded their first visits and came out gladly and inspired with a new faith in the nobility and courage to which rare men can attain—these know that the ugliness and cruelty of death were defeated. Death had no triumph, and he died as he had lived—with patience and love and submission in his heart, with the simple faith of a trustful child, and the superb gallantry of a great soul.

But even these words fail to convey the full measure of his spiritual victory. Only a few weeks before his death, the doctor-son said to his preacher-father, speaking of the spirit of unity and serenity that pervaded the entire household, "If you want to see what the Kingdom of God is like, come over to 12 Irving Street." When his father told a friend of it, he added, "Every time I come into contact with the clarity of his mind and the serenity of his spirit, I am reminded of that great saying in the New Testament, 'Death hath no more dominion over him.'"

It is lives like these that have been our most persuasive "intimations of immortality" and have themselves constituted religion's largest contribution to the immortal hope and faith. Men looking on have intuitively said of such personalities, "These must surely be the valuable and enduring structure. The bodies that helped build them can have been only a temporary scaffolding. The scaffolding may have perished as scaffoldings must, but the structure shall endure. Death cannot control them."

Nor is the quickening power of such lives limited to the time of their immediate passing. Of their *influence* also it may be truly said that death could not control them. This was obviously true of Jesus himself in most extraordinary measure. He became a far greater force in the lives of his friends and followers in the spirit than he had been when among them in the flesh: that is a plain fact of Christian history, which the New Testament not only states but by its very existence evidences. And this was not simply be-

116

cause he was a martyr who had been done to a violent and unjust death: "Men betrayed are mighty, and great are the wrongfully dead." There was and is more in it than that. On behalf of all that have shared his attitude and spirit, our intuitive conviction deepens that the universe itself would somehow betray both them and us if it were to let them cease to be. They too would then be in some deeper sense "wrongfully dead"—martyrs in a cosmic persecution. Professor George H. Palmer has put that conviction unforgettably in the closing sentence of his biography of his wife, Alice Freeman Palmer: "Though no regrets are proper for the manner of her death, who can contemplate the fact of it and not call the world irrational, if out of deference to a few particles of disordered matter it exclude so fair a spirit?"

The degree to which our beloved and honored dead not only keep, but even deepen and increase, their influence over us, in a way strangely independent of any physical presence, is a fact that soon or late falls intimately within the experience of us all. Their dear memory can touch even a common day with infinite significance, can speak with quickening power to the best within us, and lift our eyes to horizons and heights that stretch far beyond this mortal present. At the annual commemoration service of Columbia University two years ago, Dean Darrach of its medical faculty said:

The continued influence of those departed this life, and the sense of reality of the continuing existence of their personalities, has been strong enough to remove for me any doubt as to some form of life after death. What it is or in what form I care not. I believe that they continue to exist and I believe that we can be influenced by them.

Dean Darrach chose his words well. The faith in immortality cannot be proved in any conclusive sense, because the data for its demonstration (with all respect for and interest in modern psychical research) are still lacking; and even if the evidence of psychical research were much more conclusive than it seems to many of us as yet to be, the important question of the worthfulness of the life to come would still remain. Christian faith in immortality starts from the discoveries it has personally made of the worthfulness of life here and now when lived in Jesus' way, and moves on to the confidence that death can neither control nor interrupt lives that are lived that way. While it cannot be proved, it can be *lived*; and it is so lived whenever men measure their living not by time, but by quality. It is therefore always an adventure of faith, but at the same time becomes a "moral certainty." As the Swiss boy put it when a traveler asked him where Kandersteg was: he did not know, but there was the way to Kandersteg!

When Dean Willard L. Sperry last came to the University of Chicago as visiting preacher, he said that he had learned to look forward expectantly to his first glimpse of Lake Michigan from the westbound Michigan Central train. The sand dunes would first appear, with their hint of water beyond, but still shutting in the view with a wealth of interesting detail in the foreground. Presently, however, between the sandhills, a sudden far vista of shoreless blue . . . all too quickly gone . . . then for a moment glimpsed again. So, he said, is God in our human experience. And so, he might likewise have said, is

"that great water in the West
Termed Immortality"—

—stretching beyond this present that hints and yet hides it; but with the important difference that there is no railroad for this ultimate journey. Here we are each and all pioneers upon a great adventure, who cannot make a detour around this water, but must cross it for ourselves. And the only boat that will carry us over is a kind of living that we can begin to build here and now.

THE END